Daniel Worcester Faunce

Prayer as a theory and a fact

Daniel Worcester Faunce
Prayer as a theory and a fact
ISBN/EAN: 9783337283797

Printed in Europe, USA, Canada, Australia, Japan
Cover: Foto ©Thomas Meinert / pixelio.de

More available books at **www.hansebooks.com**

AS A

THEORY AND A FACT.

BY
REV. D. W. FAUNCE, D. D.

CONTENTS.

CHAPTER I.

                                         PAGE

THE POSSIBILITY OF PRAYER AS HEARD AND ANSWERED,   7

    (a.) The two beings involved.
    (b.) The intellectual relation of the two.
    (c.) The similar intellectual work.

CHAPTER II.

THE PROBABILITY OF PRAYER AS HEARD AND ANSWERED, 22

    (a.) The two beings, God and man, are both moral beings.
    (b.) They are both at work on the moral plane.

CHAPTER III.

THE LAW OF PERSONALITY IN ITS BEARING ON PRAYER, . 39

    (a.) Personality in God.
    (b.) Personality in man.
    (c.) The law calls for prayer and secures answer.

CHAPTER IV.

THE FACTOR OF SIN AS AFFECTING PRAYER, . . . 51

    (a.) It does not destroy the natural need.
    (b.) It makes it the more necessary.
    (c.) Through God's special mercy, it does not make the answer less probable.

CONTENTS.

CHAPTER V.

THE KINGDOM OF GOD AS RELATED TO PRAYER, . . 68

    (a.) It is originally arranged for prayer and its answers.
    (b.) The kingdom in the human soul.
    (c.) The kingdom in its progress in the world.
    (d.) Both these involve the natural and the supernatural.
    (e.) At every point, the work is conditioned on prayer heard and answered.

CHAPTER VI.

PRAYER AS RELATED TO NATURAL LAW, . . . 106

    (a.) Theory of original foresight and arrangement.
    (b.) Theory of a law of miracles.
    (c.) Theory of personal will.

CHAPTER VII.

NEGATIVE ANSWERS TO PRAYER ARE ACTUAL ANSWERS, . 120

    (a.) Such answers required when the petition is out of line with the dispensation.
    (b.) The divine compassion secures denial when not in accord with divine will.
    (c.) Deferred answer is not denied petition.

CHAPTER VIII.

THE REACTIONS OF SIN AS THEY INDUCE PRAYER, . . 140

    (a.) The reactions of error.
    (b.) The reactions of ages.
    (c.) The reactions of souls.

CHAPTER IX.

THE CIRCULAR MOTION OF PRAYER, ... 157

    (a.) It descends from God.
    (b.) It takes in man's voluntary petitions on its way.
    (c.) It rises again to God; since its Inspirer and its Answerer are one.

CHAPTER X.

THE LORD'S PRAYER AS OUR MODEL, ... 171

    (a.) In its arrangement.
    (b.) In its petitions.
    (c.) In its scope.
    (d.) In its spirit.

CHAPTER XI.

SUPPOSED LIMITATIONS OF PRAYER, ... 186

    (a.) From man's feebleness.
    (b.) From God's greatness.

CHAPTER XII.

PRAYER IN ITS PROPHECY, ... 201

    (a.) Its increasing volume.
    (b.) Its increasing purity.
    (c.) Its natural result.
    (d.) The ultimate man a praying man.
    (e.) The ultimate age a praying age.

PRAYER

AS A THEORY AND A FACT.

CHAPTER I.

THE POSSIBILITY OF PRAYER.

Two gentlemen were strolling leisurely by a lighted chapel into which people were passing, evidently for their weekly prayer-service. Nodding toward the open door, one of them said to the other, "Do you believe in this matter of prayer?" "Yes," was the somewhat reluctant answer, "I suppose I do, in a certain way. I think it a good thing for those who really believe in it. But," he continued, "whether there is any one at the other end of the line who does actually listen and respond, is a thing about which I am not certain." "It seems to me," replied the first speaker, "that your position is that of a man who believes in the prayer but not in the answer."

It will be the contention of this volume that all true prayer is answered. It will be claimed that this exercise of prayer involves the personal existence of two beings, God and man—one of whom offers petition, confession, worship, and thanksgiving, and the other of whom answers the petition in affirmation or in denial, receives the worship, listens to the confession, and accepts the thanksgiving.

It will be claimed that prayer is an actual and recognizable force in the universe; that, by the appointment of God, it has its place in the original scheme of things; that it has scope in God's providential plan, office in his gracious administration, authority in the promise, and confirmation in the fulfilment of God; that its negative answers are as really responses as its affirmative replies; that what men call its limitations are really extensions; that deferred answer is not denied petition; that its beginnings are with God, from whose throne its vast curve sweeps downward, passing in the lower edge of its circumference through the sphere of our voluntary petition, and thence it mounts again, curving upward, and completing the circle as it comes back to Him by whom it was first inspired and then directed and is now finally accepted; that the objections usually urged against prayer, when closely examined and freed of all misconception, are among the most potent proofs of its efficacy; that its moods and methods befit men in all the variety of their human experience on earth; and that it is a factor in producing character of such a kind that the prayers of earth, in those thus wrought upon, will antedate the praises of heaven.

The general order just outlined will be followed in this discussion.

If there were only one being in the universe, and that one being knew, or even believed, that there was no other, there could be no prayer. The one being might shout in joy or howl in anguish, but that would not be request or petition. He might try in his frenzy to impose on himself, and to act as if there were another to hear and respond, waking thereby the world's echoes. He might set himself to use all fit forms of supplication or of entreaty, under the plea of doing himself good. But all such expressions of pain or passion would come to nothing in the end. They would only react for his own harm, for he would know that he was attempting an imposition on himself, and his words would falter and freeze on his lips. Hume says, and very justly, "We can make use of no expression or even thought in prayers or entreaties which does not imply that these prayers have an influence." And we are told in the Scriptures, "He that cometh to God *must* believe that He is, and that He is the rewarder of them that diligently seek him."

The two beings, God and man, involved in this act of prayer, are, personally, minds or spirits.

In his book entitled "Primitive Culture," Edward B. Tylor gives the fit name of animism to the universal conviction that mind is distinct from matter. Assembling a vast mass of evidence in proof of his position, he says, "We must take our basis of inquiry in observation rather than in speculation; and we have to admit that the belief in spiritual beings appears among all low races with whom we have a thoroughly intimate acquaintance." Such a universal conviction among such inferior races has been called "the knowledge of God reduced to its lowest terms." But among the highest races there is also an intense conviction that another Spirit than ourselves exists. Lift the conception to its highest terms, and it gives us God.*

---

* In Timbuctoo, the natives write their prayers on the section of a tree, carrying it to a spring of water which will wash it off, and so send the prayer away. Similarly, the Thibetan pastes his prayer on a revolving cylinder and sets it in the nearest waterfall, that its face may be ever toward God. The Chinese burn gilded strips of paper and consult the ashes, as the Romans the entrails of the victims of the altar. Even the lower class of the Mohammedans, while holding to one supreme God, believe in inferior deities, and so cast their written prayers upon the bosom of their

Is this universal affirmation false or is it true?

If it be not true, or, indeed, if there be any serious doubt about its truth, the discussion must close here at the outset. For prayer is going to be vastly more than the bare recognition of a distant fact, like that of the solar spectrum in the far-away stars. A belief that God *is*, is fundamental. His existence must not be a speculation to us, nor an indistinct inference. He is not a universally diffused ether, or a shapeless phantom, or an impersonality, or a force, or an essence, but the actual personal God, if we are going to pray to Him and get from Him an answer.

No less must the fact be established for ourselves that we are actual persons. The validity of the evidence for man as an individual must be undisputed. Happily, here doubt is impossible. For the instant question, when man says that he doubts, is this, "What is it that doubts, and who

---

sacred river, holding that the god of the waters is great enough to ward off the approach of disease.

And over against these lowest populations it would be easy to cite the most eminent men, some of them not Christian believers, who own a God. "I have lived," said Benjamin Franklin, in the convention for forming a Constitution, "for a long time, and the longer I live the more convincing proofs I see of this truth, that God governs the affairs of man. I therefore beg leave to move that henceforth prayers imploring the assistance of heaven on our deliberations be held in this assembly every morning before we proceed to business."

is it that asks the question?" "I *think*, therefore I *am*" is an argument which thousands feel and rest upon with absolute certainty, who could not put their conviction into logical statement.

> "The baby, new to earth and sky,
> What time his tender palm is pressed
> Against the circle of the breast,
> Has never thought that "this is I."
> But as he grows, he gathers much,
> And learns the use of "I" and "me,"
> And finds "I am not what I see,
> I'm other than the things I touch."
> So rounds he to a separate mind,
> From whence clear memory may begin,
> As through the frame that binds him in
> His isolation grows defined."

When plain men wish to express the utmost degree of conviction, they say, "I am as certain of that thing as that I exist."

All logical minds must have similar powers. Exceedingly unlike may be the degree, but the powers must be enough alike to work on the same logical plane. So far as we can understand, the highest mode of intelligence is connected with reasoning powers. The reasonable is of higher grade than the instinctive. All minds made up so as to use reason, must be similar in make and in working. They must work on the plane of "the true and the false." All things in the intellectual sphere are measured by that one plumb-line. In this realm of the logical, the realm measured by this one rule of "the true and the false," we do our work, and the highest worker in this realm we call *God*. Dropping, here and now, that we may the better take them up by-and-by, all those convictions usually termed "moral" and "spiritual," holding now to the word spiritual only in its merely intellectual sense, we may just glance a moment or two, less to increase our confidence and more to realize our impression, at the way in which we come to be obliged, in this logical realm, to believe in our God.

There is a quick, sharp argument that satisfies most men. It is this. A designer will manifest design in his work. Evidences of designing are everywhere about us, in earth, in air, in sky; are seen equally in things, and in the law of them; are obvious in forces, and in the way they are made to work; in tendencies, and the ends toward which they are developing; in these minds so made up as to refer in every case a design to a designing mind, a plan to a planning mind, a universal plan of things to a universally existing and planning mind—and this mind is God. The statement of the proposition is, to many persons, the best proof, for it is to them nearly or quite self-evident.

It has indeed been said in reply that the argument from design proves a very grand and supernatural being, who, since he is the highest being we can know, deserves our recognition, reverence, and worship. He is Creator, Sustainer, Sovereign Ruler over all we know. But it is urged that he need not be the Absolute God; that the argument goes very far but does not fully and, at the last point, actually reach so far up as to prove the One Ever-living and Eternal God. Why not, say some, own this designer, architect, worker, just a little short of the Sovereign God? Few will see the difference; yet some would claim that there might be a flaw in some far-up link of the chain. Suppose we admit it. Then we have this to say, that when we have gone up as far as our reason can go, there is a round out of sight, a final round of our ladder not quite discernible; but that with every step in our climbing, so far from the prize eluding us, we have grown in the conviction that God is there, that in that direction lies the infinite trend of things and the final goal of thought. Indeed, for some minds this trend of things is the best possible proof of God. The line of approach is better than any supposed finite culmination.

But the two ways of reaching the same conviction are not in themselves really antagonistic. They are methods suited to unlike minds. The broad way of our human reason is wide enough to admit upon it many paths, some of which run nearer, it may be, to the middle of the course than others, but all of which are within the happy limiting lines that bound the truth. There are minds so constituted that a grand *trend* is more convincing than the sight of the ultimate goal. Inclosed in the circular box men call a compass is a delicate needle, which, however you disturb it, trembles back to its pole. And it does this because all over the earth run unseen magnetic currents converging toward an unseen magnetic centre far away in the North. And men sail on every ocean of the world, and measure their land on every continent of the round globe, by that little needle that follows the trend of those magnetic currents toward the pole. But, then, no mortal foot ever touched that pole, no mortal eye ever saw it. It is, the world over, *only a trend*. And yet on that trend rests all the science of navigation and all the science of mensuration. And not only the earth beneath, but the wide heavens are marked out and mapped off in lines of gigantic boundary by that steady trend toward a pole that no man has ever seen or touched. The trend toward God in all forms of human thought is just as distinct. And he is as unreasonable who would destroy all the fair fabric of modern sciences, celestial and terrestrial, because no human foot has as yet touched that pole, as he who denies the culminating point of all religious trend because his reason cannot put its logical finger on his God.

Paley's argument for design, founded on the watch supposed to be discovered on a heath, and by the finder to be accounted for, has served its purpose in the form in which he gave it. Men then were considering the facts simply and only, and from these alone Paley's inference was strictly logical. The watch had a maker. But now that both facts and the law of them are matters for consideration, the inference of a designing mind, so far from being weakened, is every way broadened and strengthened. The design runs back as far as the law is seen to exist. The further the line of development, and the wider the range of the laws under which that development is seen to have taken place, the larger is the design, the greater the wisdom and power that are manifested, and the stronger the argument for a God. Instead of the one fact, you have now to consider the thousand previous facts that led up to it, and the longer the line of the development, the more remarkable becomes the design of the designing mind. For law is only method, in accordance with which fact comes into notice. The larger the play of the forces, and the more complex their working, the more the need of control, lest they destroy the development.

Says another, "Since we find that these forces can be controlled by us within certain limits, the most reasonable conclusion seems to be that they (these laws) are connected with another Will, 'in whom is no variableness,' and who is 'the same yesterday, to-day, and forever.'"

When Mansel argued that the Infinite One must be the Unknowable One, and yet strove vainly to escape from the consequence of his remorseless logic, it only needed that some one should point out the wide difference between comprehending God and apprehending him. On the shore of the ocean one may feel the salt sea breeze as it fans his cheek, and may taste the spray that loads the air, and may mark the white-winged ships, flying the flags of all nationalities, and in this way may apprehend clearly and certainly the fact that the vast body of water on which he is looking is the ocean, even though he knows that his vision cannot comprehend its breath, nor take in the sight of the continents beyond its rolling waste of waves.

And those who claim to have rational intuition of God are not to be overlooked, either in the goodly number of them or the intellectual force they carry. It is claimed that the idea of God is involved in the very process of our human thinking; that every thought is an inquiry for a cause, and so comprehends in it the final idea of a First or a Chief Cause; that all right thinking involves a Standard Thinker; that God is involved in all thought, just as is self-hood; that God is the "Alter Ego," as the thinker is himself the "Ego." Thus, when we are born, we are ushered into a scheme of things already existing, where one finds that the great distinction between the "true and the false" is not established by us, but is a perpetual existence—made so by the Eternal Mind. So that it becomes as true of mind as of body, that in God "we live and move and have our being." And thus we find the intellectual plane on which we meet God and "can think over his thoughts." And meeting on this plane, we see the possibility of two beings like God and man so entering into a relation with each other that the one can give answer to the other's prayer.

And it has also been urged that the human mind is constituted in such a way as to be receptive to the idea of the One Living and True God; that we are so made up intellectually as to be in waiting for the idea; that the idea finds anticipations and preparations for it in our nature; that the suggestion of it, from whatsoever source, finds a readiness of response that amounts to an affinity for it; that, whether it rises out of the soul within, born of the lower consciousness, or starts out of our emotional nature to be afterward received and justified by the intellect, it is always presented to the mind; that everywhere man is constitutionally fitted to know God, and so by every avenue of his being, mental and moral, he is made up to apprehend the fact that lies at the basis of all facts, that *God is*.

To still others, the genesis of the idea is in the correlative demands of the nature alike of God and of man. God is, as they say, the complement truth to man's being. God has need of some such being to bless and love, a being with whose welfare he can charge himself, and whose prayer he can hear; a being outranking angels, with powers for understanding in some degree his works, and his providence, and his Word. So that, "Let us make man," is the expression of a yearning for a being of high moral grade, "made in the image of God." And in turn man, in his dependence, needs God's help and sustenance; and in his littleness, needs God's greatness. Man is made to cling and clasp, as the vine its oak. He is never centred in self, but is to be centred in God. God is the cap-stone of man's thought, as well as the supply for the yearning of man's heart. As the earth needs a sun and was made for it, so the sun needs an earth to shine upon. The craving for God in our human nature must have been put there by him who is at once its source and its supply. And all this proves, at least, the *possibility* of prayer. Not now to urge more than this, it must be granted that there is room for the belief. It is clearly in the range of possible things that the two beings should interchange thought and care, man bringing his word of prayer, and God his word of revelation. There is enough in these indications to induce hope that it may be so. The idea of God, and of such a God, is strong in some minds in this way of complementary supply for a craving that can find no other satisfaction.

These various ways of seizing with the logical reason on this idea of God are by no means mutually exclusive of each other; and they are so far from contradictory that they are the rather helpful. Their trend is in one direction. And it is to be expected that this universal idea of God will pervade all our faculties, and the whole nature of man be hospitable thereto. All these various ways of looking are in one direction. A man may stand at the foot of the Bunker Hill

Monument, and look up its slant sides, putting by turns his eye to each. He seems to touch the sky with his vision. He does not actually do that. *But the sky is that way.* He is looking in that direction. He knows that somewhere, far above the monument, those lines in his eye reach an apex, and that any one of them, continued on, would strike the sky. To many minds, and they are among our surest mental workers, there are no such strong proofs, in any matter, as are these of trend, and direction, and convergence. The fact that various minds approach the idea from so many positions is reassuring. Such men feel that they are treading, when they go over all these various arguments, along the lines of the grandest thought, and are walking safely. The best thinking must be ever "thinking over again the thoughts of God." These souls, in the completeness of their own satisfaction with the argument, might not be content with claiming a mere inference as to the *possibility* of prayer. They would insist upon a stronger inference. But let us be modest in our claim at this point of the discussion. Let us claim only that even the sceptic must allow that there is a mighty trend toward the belief that it is possible for God to hear and answer prayer.

CHAPTER II.

THE PROBABILITY OF PRAYER.

We have seen which way lie the possibilities on this question of answered prayer.

It is now to be urged that the immense *probabilities* run in the same direction. The argument has been along the line of the actual existence of the two beings involved in this exercise of prayer. God and man have been seen as related, since they are working, intellectually, on the same "plane of the true and the false," and are using similar though unequal powers, by which they can seek a common result.

But these two beings are also workers on another plane—that of the spiritual life.

It is to be noticed that both God and man are supernatural factors in securing results; and so they are both, by virtue of their rank of being, capable of working over and above, as well as in and through, those things which we call "natural." For free actors have a certain power of personal force. They are capable of initiating action where it did not exist before. They originate. They put into exercise a new force. They thrust in a new energy, which is outside of "nature" and in addition thereto; it is the self-originating force of will. It is sometimes conceived of less as the exercise of a single faculty, and more as an act of the mind itself, using itself executively. And this kind of force is entirely unlike those powers with which physical objects are supposed to be equipped. In man, physical brain-force and mental will-power are parallel facts, and for that very reason are not identical. They exist together, and one is as is the other; and therefore the one is not the other. Says Tyndall, "We can trace the development of a nervous system (in man), and can correlate it with the parallel phenomena of sentient thought. Parallelism without contact is implied; but there is no fusion possible between the two classes of facts." So elsewhere Tyndall says, "Thought and sentiment are accompanied doubtless by movements in the molecules of the brain, but the mode of connection between the two is simply to us unthinkable. The connection between mind and matter is not necessary but empirical." In some way, we know not and need not to know how, this will-power touches the physical in man's body, and the touch proves them utterly unlike. Body and mind have not a quality in common. In the physical realm there is the "natura," and in the spiritual realm there is the "super-natura;" the two, in the case of man, are singularly conjoined, and as singularly separated. There is just enough of resemblance and relation between the facts and forces of the physical world and those of the spiritual world to warrant very careful and discriminating analogy. To confound the facts or laws of the two is to destroy both realms for us as objects of thought and inquiry. If Prof. Drummond, in his popular work, "Natural Law in the Spiritual World," is held to have proved the laws of the two realms to be analogous rather than identical, he will have done service to science by rendering it more intelligible to thousands of plain readers, and none the less service to religion by showing that its facts have both parallel and illustration in the physical world.

It must be admitted that God, one of these free and supernatural factors, *could* have so arranged the original scheme of things as to provide for hearing and answering prayer. The contrary can be maintained only on some theory that denies the divine sovereignty. It has been alleged that existing arrangements show no place open for such things as answers to prayer. But does any man know all the existing arrangements? To assume that God *could* not, because he *has* not, so far as some men can see, arranged for answered prayer, is not only poor logic, but it is the assumption of omniscience. For if there be one fact or force unknown, one arrangement not understood, one purpose of God not disclosed to this objector, then the one undiscovered force, the one unrevealed purpose, may be the very thing needed to answer all objections, and to show God abundantly able and willing to do this thing. It is hard to believe that a free being would have so imprisoned himself in his own universe that he should not be able to listen to the great cry that in all ages would come up into his ears from man, the creature made in his own image. Able to make the arrangement through his original plan of nature, in the absence of any conflicting reasons, is it not probable that, as our loving God, he would have so ordered facts and forces that room would be secured for the answer of prayer?

And the probability increases when we consider the peculiar duality and yet unity of the known and visible universe which God has made. For the actual universe, so far as we can understand it, presents itself as having both a spiritual and a physical world, and the one the counterpart of the other. Thought is greater than thing, but thing is conformed to thought. Long ago Herschel pointed out the fact that the atoms of which the visible universe is composed have on them the stamp of being manufactured articles; that the unseen is indicated by the seen and dominated thereby in purpose; that the natural world must have a beginning in time and would have an ending; and that, when it ends, it will leave behind it that unseen world whence came its idea and existence, and to the more central facts of which it is conformed, as vesture to the body it clothes. The natural is the illuminated dial plate, all the figures of which are visible to us only because of the light behind it. So that the natural and the spiritual worlds are to be conceived of as constituting, when taken together, the one universe of God. If the physical part of it be regarded as placed under the fixed law of the necessary, the other part is to be deemed under the correlated law of the personal and the free. The material world has its objects with such qualities as hardness and softness, color and weight. But none the less has the spiritual world its objects, having qualities such as memory and will, love and hate. It is the realm where "the law of the right and the wrong" is just as really a law as is gravity in the physical world. This spiritual world has its facts of God and the soul, of conscience and commandment, of obedience and disobedience, of probation and immortality. We do not *make* the physical world with its objects and forces and laws. We are born into it in body. It was here before we came. We simply accept it as an arrangement of God appointed for our physical position. We take it as ready-made to our hand, and do our work amid these facts and forces which we find adapted to our mortal life. In the same way we are born into the mental realm. It is the realm of the knowable. It has its facts and laws. Its great law, fundamental as is gravity in the physical realm, is "the law of the true and the false." We do not *make* a thing true or false. It is so, outside of ourselves or our decisions. We simply recognize it as such, and act upon it. We do not make the standard by which we judge things. We find this law of the true and the false in the world when we come; we find it used by men, and we accept it. It is a system of things that we did not originate, but into the midst of which we are thrust to do our mental work in life. Exactly as it is with the physical and mental realms, so is it with the moral realm. We are thrust into the midst of its facts; and they are as real as are those of the physical or the intellectual world. It has its own objects, its own forces, and its own laws. It is the realm where reigns "the law of the right and the wrong," exactly as in the intellectual sphere we have "the law of the true and the false." No man makes anything right or wrong. It is so in itself. It was so before we came, and would be so if we were out of the system. It is the world where, by virtue of our moral equipment of faculties, we do our work, exactly as by our physical equipment of hand and foot and eye and ear we do our physical work. Physical material is, in our physical world, just what moral material is in our spiritual world. Physical facts are our environment in body, as spiritual facts are the furnishing for our spiritual life. They are not it. It demands them. Intellectual truth for the sentient mind, and moral truth for the conscious soul, are the requirements of faculty, just as is light for the eye and an objective world for the sense of touch.

As to the rank of these three realms, the physical world, the intellectual world, and the moral world—it is to be noticed that the latter has some deliverance to offer upon each of the other realms besides its own. The final ends of God are moral ends; and God and man both have it to use the physical and the mental so as to secure moral results. Prayer in its askings and answerings will have to do mainly with the moral realm; for the soul's duties and trials, its perplexities and weaknesses, its sins and its sorrows, its struggle and its salvation, are the main things about which prayer is concerned. And yet the physical often bears so closely on the moral that we ask for material things as they are related to our spiritual life.

Dr. Bushnell, after urging that matter is not a two-faced something, one face of which is physical and the other spiritual, insists that "God has in fact erected another and higher system—that of spiritual government—for which nature exists." But as the two worlds are related, and prayer may have to do with them both, the answer may come in the related realm rather than that concerning which we specifically ask. But by far the larger number of requests will be within the spiritual sphere of things. Our prayer-tests will be mainly in the moral realm, where lie our largest needs, and to which come the promises that are of grandest scope. In this moral realm, it is soul meeting soul, the essential man meeting the One in whom his largest desires find their satisfaction. Both act under the law of sympathetic touch; and the prayer would seem to be not more natural than the answer. It is heart drawn to heart. It is a moral act in which two spiritual beings, in moral agreement, and acting on the same moral plane, speak to each other of their moral work. What more natural than that the one should ask, and the other give, counsel; that the weaker in right should seek help of the stronger; that recognition should pass into communion of thought and feeling, in those who, however far apart in position, are seeking a common moral end? Is there anything improbable in such an exercise? Surely there should be an arrangement by which, at least occasionally, and in the great crises of a man's life, this thing might be done. We can certainly maintain it as a very strong probability that it is done. It is more than likely that somewhere and somehow, at least in the interspaces of event and law, if in no other way, God has left himself room for answer to the petitions of those so evidently made in his own image. What if, by-and-by, further on in the argument, we shall find that God is shut up to no such narrow limits as some might think; that there is no reason to ask how, under and between physical laws, there can be crevice and loophole, so that God can find place to send answer to human petition; but that, alike by abundant arrangement, both in the physical and spiritual realms, and by his own ever-present personality, he is able, from the depths of his being, to sound the depths of our souls, when he has encouraged and inspired the prayer he proposes to answer?

Or yet again: this question of the probability

of answered petition can be approached from the physical side. We can begin at the other end of the line and come in toward the centre. It adds to the force of the argument to recall the conceded physical fact that even the words spoken by man, in oath as well as in prayer, make for themselves an imperishable record. Prayer is thus a part of the ever-written literature of the universe, remaining visible for the inspection of God and for the review of other moral beings with finer perceptions—perhaps for the continuous reading of man himself in superior states of development. Says another, "The air is one vast library, on whose pages are forever written all that man has ever said, or woman ever whispered." "The earth and the sea give up their dead" in ways beyond those in which our interpretation may have understood the words. What we have written we have written. And the voice of prayer can be no exception, for even its words are not lost. Addressed, prayer goes to its destination. The petition of the devout heart has clothed itself in words; those words take their place among the facts that cannot be changed or lost. The universe is like one of those old-time palimpsests, or manuscripts covered over with successive layers of writing, which now, by our modern skill, are taken off separately and read out in the audience of the world, and whosoever cares may listen. There is an instrument into which you may speak, and, instantly, on a cylinder, not only your words, but your tones, your stress and accentuation, are all preserved, and the cylinder will give it all back again with absolute fidelity and startling distinctness; and that not once or twice, but an unknown number of times. The universe may be considered as one vast and indestructible graphophone, which records all that man has ever said, and returns all the utterances he has ever made, even the most secret prayer that has ever left his lips in the chamber of his devotion. To ask is to answer the poet's question:

> " Do the elements subtle reflection give?
> Do pictures of all ages live
> On nature's infinite negative?"

In a universe with a recording system so perfect, a telegraphic system so carefully arranged and reaching so far with every word entrusted to its care, can a single sentence of human supplication get out of the range of God's eye or ear? Can he be the kind of a being who is not likely to listen kindly and answer fully the petition which is a perpetual fact? It rises from an earnest soul, it bursts the bounds of the lips and breaks into a vocal prayer, which thenceforth becomes an imperishable fact in the universe of God. It must be so, or prayer is the great exception. If united to the words there is also the glowing thought, so that the soul as well as the body of the prayer is to come up and stand before God, and if he is then to shut his ear, surely that separate and unrelated fact should be shown. Then, and only then, will we admit, however reluctantly, that though the trend of all things else is toward the belief in answered prayer, yet for some good reason deeply hid in the heart of God, he does not listen and will not respond to our cry. But we are not forced to any such painful conclusion. There is no proof that prayer is the sad exception. It cannot be that while an oath is recorded, a prayer makes such slight record as to be quickly obliterated. The Omniscient must know when we pray. He will not vacate his omniscience by refusing to regard any such fact as prayer. God cannot, being God, but hear, even if he did not wish to listen. He is in the room where you pray. He could not possibly be absent. He holds up the earth beneath you. Each object in the room, the floor on which you kneel, the chair, table, or bed against which your hand rests, are all kept in existence and in form by him. "By him all things consist;" *i. e.*, stand as they stand. It is his present energy, there and then exercised, that keeps all things in being and works all laws.

He must at least hear, if he does not answer. But the immense probability is that, going so far as to hear, he will take the one step more, that of choosing to *answer* the suppliant's petition.

Further: such an arrangement for hearing would obviously be a good arrangement. It would provide for God's manifestation of himself and for man's development in the highest lines of religious living. It certainly would not be dishonorable to God, and as certainly would be helpful to man. It would seem to open a way for God to disclose his will and direct our mortal life, which would not be omitted by one who, as a worker on the same moral plane, must care for our welfare in caring for himself and his own plans.

It is true that a crude interpretation of some few texts of Scripture, under pretence of magnifying prayer, has really left God no room to answer. Under the effort to exalt God's promise, it has really discrowned God himself. Good men, pleading that the words "whatsoever ye shall ask" are unlimited—an error which would have been avoided by study of the context—have made God vacate sovereignty in their behalf; have not even left him the poor liberty to deny them any wish or whim; have regarded him as yielding to them, through his unlimited promise, the control of events. If their view is correct, they are sovereigns, and he is the subject who is to do what they may say when they ask anything in prayer. But we are not told that we may mount the throne in our "whatsoever ye ask;" only that this is the liberty we have, to ask what we will of strength and direction for work in which we seek that "the Father may be glorified in the Son."* Prayer is not human whim, but holy desire offered up for things according to the will of God. It is not a man imposing his test on God, but God proposing the line along which, in his promises, we may prove him. Prayer sees him always on the throne to grant or to deny, answering equally in either case. It never discrowns the God it addresses. Let no man think the less of true prayer for that rashness of interpretation which, under color of honoring prayer, is really dishonorable to God.

On the other hand, could one imagine any exercise more adapted to ennoble man than this of true prayer? It would promote that genuine humility which consists well with the highest exaltation. It lifts mind and heart toward him who is the sum of all excellence. We imitate whom we worship. We grow like him whom we adore. We are ourselves exalted in exalting him. It

---
* See John, xiv. 13, 14.

stands to reason that no man can be a worse man, but on the contrary a better man, for entering daily his closet and praying to his Father and his God. Prayer tends to make the relations we sustain to God more definite. It is an act that is between himself and our central selves. It is called "drawing near to God." The sense of the Divine Being as one ever present may grow dull elsewhere, but it becomes sharp again in the closet. Prayer vitalizes the best truths. It refines the ore of Christian doctrine and leaves behind the true gold. Truth that can be prayed is truth that is newly tested and minted. The creed that ministers to true prayer is thereby the proven creed. We see further into spiritual truth on our knees than when standing highest on our feet. Heart then leads head, as it was made to do. If God has an arrangement for hearing and answering prayer, it must tend to vitalize all his best truths for us. In this way he can get himself believed with a profound and living faith. It would be, if he has chosen prayer as a fact in his universe, a sort of continuous authentication of revelation; not indeed by way of adding new truths, but by vivifying those that are already known. For if prayer and its answer are correlated facts, they are also related facts to other things in the supernatural realm of God and souls.

The great facts of revelation go well with this exercise of prayer. They do indeed bear on themselves the brand of miraculous signature and indorsement. But they are centuries away from us. They cannot be repeated; since, if frequent, the miracles attesting them would cease to be authentications. And they are in danger, because of their infrequence, less of being denied than unused as proofs of divine utterances. They and the truths indorsed by them, are in danger of lying useless on the surface of one's belief, the spiritual side of the miracles neglected, and their moral worth as divine object lessons not duly estimated. What is needed is some such exercise as prayer which shall put a man's soul into moral mood, so that the Christian facts shall have a fair chance in their double appeal to heart and to head; so that from the vantage ground of a profound moral sympathy these facts shall have the kind of reception to which they are entitled. The separating centuries will depart and the full force of these truths not be weakened by distance in time. We need to be put into close communion with them. Prayer would do this thing for those generations of men which, like our own, are necessarily separated from those occurrences. Prayer would find these facts at their due strength. It would bring them back in their hallowed freshness. In that case the Bible would feed the flame of prayer, and prayer give new vividness to the Bible. There would be the "threefold cord not easily broken." There would be the Bible received on its own evidence; next, prayer as a matter of testimony from praying men; and then there would be also the agreement of the two, as a third evidence to be added to the others.

So that for his own glory as well as for our good, for the interests of truth as well as of righteousness, God may be considered as not likely to have omitted to furnish an arrangement for answering human prayer; as not likely to have made no provision for what would be of such obvious and inestimable worth to himself and to all that moral realm over which he is sovereign, and the success of which he has charged himself to secure. Prayer would seem to be a fit thing to be included in his original scheme of things, a holy and wise fore-ordination of God.

These growing probabilities approach very near the edge of certainty. Starting from so many points in the circumference, they run always in such a direction that we cannot but know what is the centre of the circle.

CHAPTER III.

PERSONALITY AS A LAW.

It is a fine remark of Stirling that "a man is free because he obeys motives." This leaves the person behind the motive, who selects and acts upon it, as the chief factor. There is a law of personality. Individual force is a fact and a power in the universe, as really as is gravity. Men inquire how natural laws can be used or can be set aside in the answering of prayer. But personality is a consideration quite as important as physical law or material fact. For a large part of human life consists in matching human will against material obstacles. We manage to have our way, and practically to override physical law a thousand times a day. Law would keep a man's foot fast to the earth where it is set. But his will is thrust in as the new superior and personal force, and he lifts the foot, accomplishing thereby what amounts to the same thing, in result, as a suspension of the law of gravity. Every voluntary movement of the body tramples on the law. We overwork it. We combine the law of gravity with other laws, and so come inventions that save expenditure of human force. The law is there, but we are its masters, coercing it, managing it, combining it, opposing it. It is stable, and therefore we depend upon it. In a universe with unstable laws the human will could do nothing at all. Says Prof. Momrie in his work on "Personality," "Our life is spent in using, adapting, combining, and controlling the forces of the material world. And all this we achieve not in spite of, but because of, the inviolability of law." If man can do all this, cannot God do more? If he shall fail to do more in order to make room for answering prayer, will he not put himself down to a position lower than that taken by man? We must ourselves, in our thinking, make room for God's personality in all else; and why not then in prayer? The argument here and now grounds itself on this very inviolability of nature which makes these exercises of personality manifest in God as in man. "Consciousness," says Prof. Momrie, "is the knowledge which we have of ourselves, *along with our states.*" This last clause is a very happy addition to the usual definition given by Bain, Hamilton, Spencer, and McCosh; and it answers Mill and the whole Positivist school in a single member of a sentence. But this consciousness is aware of its own essential power. We know ourselves as sending out the energy of a personal will. We know that this is the volition of a free being. We act as out of self. How much more must God do so! And hence his scope of activity in answering prayer.

But personality has more to do than any other one thing that can be named in securing answers to requests. You ask a favor of a fellow-man. It is clearly within his power to grant it. The likelihood of his granting it depends almost entirely on his personality—on that assemblage of tastes and wishes and preferences which make up his disposition as a man; on the individual element in him; on the known ends he has in life; on the request as one which such a man as he would be likely to consider; on his friendship for you; on the whole sum of your relations to him as he understands them. And you, in view of all these personal considerations, form your judgment of his probable answer to your request. The personal element controls. And why is it not so with God, as the one to whom we put up our prayers? We are warranted in giving very large room to this particular element.

Nor is personality so uncertain a thing that we cannot count upon it. So far from this, we estimate personality at a given worth every day of our lives in dealing with others. So far from unreliable, it is a matter of exact calculation—as much so as any physical law. For what we call the laws of material nature depend for their certainty solely on the firm personal will of God. He keeps them as they are. If we can rely on them, it is only because there is a reliable mind back of them. But even freedom has its law, and may be duly estimated. Personality has its force, on which we can reckon. Individuality has its mode of action, which can be ascertained. The free will works under its own law, and it is as is the mind and heart of the actor. Its law is unlike that in the material world; but it is as capable of being ascertained and tabulated as is gravity. An infinite mind could make no mistake in forecasting what a man or a whole race of men would do under given circumstances. And a finite mind would approximate to correctness just in proportion to its knowledge of facts and of men and the balance of its judgment. There is a philosophy of history; and this because we have learned that we can depend upon the free action of free agents in a given condition.

Only notice very carefully that this is not the kind of certainty which comes from the equal and even pressure of physical law upon material atoms. For there is a kind of bound and rebound in the free human will, which, however, is also in turn a thing for calculation. So that we can sit down with the history of man, exactly as does the scientist with his materials in the laboratory, and we can compute the volume and direction of united or contrasted personalities. French characteristics being what they are, we are fairly sure that in a given set of circumstances Frenchmen will do this or that thing. Englishmen, having definite traits of character, will act out their united personality, and we reckon definitely on their conduct. Not chemical affinity is more sure to act in nature than these traits of nationality to secure action of a definite social, political, or religious kind. Such laws of personality override all others, and the disposition of a people is a stronger factor, within its proper sphere, than is that physical environment of which naturalists have so much to say.

Where personality has room to act there is shown the wide difference between physical "necessity" and moral "certainty." Two remarkable lines of intervention are manifest in human history, both showing the superiority of rank in the moral sphere. One is the rise and sweep of forces, social, political, and religious, across the sea of human thought and feeling; the other is the rise of single personalities here and there which sway men almost regally—a single great soul affecting profoundly millions of other souls. Of the former class are those great tidal waves of feeling that roll over the moral ocean and dash themselves against every shore. There have been the uprisings of a great people in favor of freedom; the singular incitement to better forms of public manners and morals; the sudden revivals of temperance, of thrift, of prudential saving, of commercial enterprise, and of spiritual religion. And these great movements in human thought have shown the difference between steady mechanical law and that spiritual force which is generated in the higher sphere. The Infinite Mind can rouse these tides on this wide sea and direct their movement, or can calm these surges at will. Personality in God can act through these moral forces that so sway nations; and, inciting a people to pray, he can so guide these consenting personalities that not only great masses of men, but the most retired human souls, shall be prepared for auspicious answers. Prayer may thus be God's breath alike in petition and response; and God's sway of these mighty forces will sometimes seem to men so unlike those he uses in the material world, that thinking men shall feel more certain of an answer to prayer than if it came only through the working of physical law.

And the appearance here and there on the

wide theatre of human events of some great soul whose personality sways other personalities, yet without destroying at all their individual freedom, is another of those striking facts which show how unlike are the physical and the moral realms. They indicate the whole wide world of influences amid which God also, by his will, can work without hindrance from material law. They give us a glimpse of the wide scope in which the Divine Personality can accomplish desired results. They show how, his hand on all things, he can make a way for the answer of prayer. If man can do so much in securing moral results, what cannot God accomplish amid these free agents, who, doing their own will, are often unconsciously bringing about his purposes? The rise of such a man as Cyrus, whose career is the standing marvel of history; of Alexander, whose sword was a ploughshare, turning the world-furrow into which there dropped the swiftly springing seeds of Greek thought; of Napoleon in these later years, the man whose conquests and whose code changed the map of Europe and the jurisprudence of its nations—these are instances of the prodigious force of personality. Nor are all the stars that dot this firmament of disastrous portent. There are those of happy omen and blessed light. Think of that greatest man of the olden time—

a praying soul was his—that Moses, who stamped his image and superscription upon his people so deeply that though they are without a king or a capital, wandering evermore in the wilderness of the world, they remain a nation separated from all others. The birth-mark of the Hebrew Moses is ineffaceable. But if this man was the select soul, more potent in influence than any other in the olden centuries, who can be named to match him in the Christian era for moral impression and leadership? There is one man, just within the boundary lines of the new dispensation. He too is a praying man. The great apostle has so shaped the thought and action of men that some have been tempted to call our religion less that of Jesus and more that of Paul. If Moses was the great legislator whose system of jurisprudence rules, in its essential principles, the civilized world to-day, none the less must we claim for Paul that he set his mark through his Epistles so distinctly on the Christian world that the creeds of Christendom can ask nothing higher than to be called "Pauline" in theology. But this man Paul claimed in turn for himself that he was simply an apostle of the risen Son of God. Each of these men, Moses and Paul, had it for a characteristic that he was a praying man. The great lawgiver fell on his face before God, and the apostle bows his knee to the Father of our Lord Jesus Christ. And so these two men, not only by genius of a higher order, but by devotion rapt and intelligent, became the two most influential men who have ever trod the planet. Now comes the simple question: Can men sway souls like this, and is God excepted from doing as much as they? Can they do masterful deeds, sway men who are still free agents so amazingly, and is God to act less royally? They heard the words of human call and answered in potent language; and shall not God hear the cry of men, and sway the race in reply thereto? Of all personalities, that of God must be most pronounced. Paul uses a word which has in it the divine personality. It is the word "grace." It means that profound kindness which is in the heart of God toward men, and is exhibited in the gift and gospel of his Son Jesus Christ. God's "grace" is the beating heart, the overflow of the divine yearning for man's welfare. It is his peculiar personality in its exercise toward the human race. Human love can conquer vast obstacles. It is wonderful in its working. But "God so loved the world that he gave his only-begotten Son." "Don't you think it was wonderful that God so loved us?" said one in the presence of a little child. "I think it was just like him," replied the little theologian. God is indeed Ruler, and he will be our final Judge. The judicial element in every man is a part of his moral personality. It must exist also in God. But he is the merciful and forbearing Ruler and Judge. By his deepest nature he is loath to condemn. By disposition he is inclined to mercy. He delights in love. Even a kindly judge will speak out in answer to an appealing word; and though sometimes he must decline to answer favorably a request, he will at least answer. A kindly father will not pass by the cry of his child in silence. I argue prayer from the heart of God; from the deepest thing in the disposition of God; from all the revelations of the personality of God; from the liberty and the love of God.

If it were worth while to press the argument from probability further, there might be named the law of sympathetic environment. Souls very far apart in volume may yet be like-minded. The same atmosphere may be vital to each. The native Christian air is one in which desires soar, as birds with wings. The life in the lung draws the vital air, and then in turn is vitalized thereby. The soul's humble breathings of desire find an ear that hears them, since they gratify its own longings. The asking soul and the answering Lord are both in the same kingdom—the one as a subject, the other as a sovereign. The kingdom of God is a kingdom of thought. "His thoughts are great to us-ward." But thought seeks its expression; the speaker his hearer; the God his man; the man his God. To meet environment is the craving of mind. There is room for mutual communication of thought. The Bible speaks of "my thoughts" and of "your thoughts." There is room for this moral exchange, for this touch of moral personality, for this individualism in petition and in response. "Ask—for every one that asketh receiveth," is simply the doctrine of moral response; or, put into the phrase of the physical realm, it is what bound and rebound are in material things. The one true, the other must be. Man's yearnings lifted God-ward meet the descending answer fresh from the opening heart of his God. Such environment involves moral exchange. The praying man and the responding God are seeking a common moral end. The king has subjects. But these subjects are "sons of God." Shall the members of a united household hold no intercourse? What if we agree to designate that intercourse as prayer and its answer?

A warranted inference from this immense probability of answered prayer is that of revelation. Convinced that prayer is a duty, the next thing is the desire to be taught how to pray.

The Bible and prayer are twin facts. The probability of the one as the companion of the other is very great. The reasonableness of prayer, and, equally, the reasonableness of a divine revelation, are felt by millions of the race. It is plain that the religion that can hold the world in all coming centuries must be the religion of authentic documents. It must be a book of former revelations, an Old Testament. But an Old Testament demands a New Testament. It must be a book of man's making, along the line of human literature, and yet on it, for authority, there must be set the seal of God's inspiration. Such a book goes well with the idea of prayer. And when such a book throws wide its pages, we find not only direct promises and specific examples, but the whole tone of the book, the key-note, to which all its song is pitched, is that of prayer offered and answer given. Its very praises are prayers; its epistles are interrupted with outburst and overflow of prayer; so that the Bible is the prayer-book of the world.

CHAPTER IV.

SIN AS A FACTOR IN THE QUESTION OF PRAYER.

So far we have considered man as man in his ethical nature. He craves God normally, as God him.

But there must come now into the discussion a new element—that of human *sin;* and we must inquire how this new factor affects the question of prayer as offered and as answered. Will sin shut God's ear? On the other side, will sin hinder man's prayer?

We must remember that our ethical nature remains, even though subjected now to a sinning heart. It is as when some royal personage has been seized upon and thrust down into a dungeon, under the very palace in the throne-room of which he once reigned. Sin is the usurping servant who abides not by any right in the palace built for the Son.* The glory of the ethical nature may be obscured, but never be destroyed, by the wrong voluntary nature. For the ethical nature, the nature that is shown in the possession

---

* John, viii. 35.

of conscience and right reason, is an imperishable part of ourselves. Its yearnings may be for a time, but only for a time, suppressed. They will find their utterance. The cry of the royal prisoner is sometimes heard. It comes up into the court of the usurper, and the guilty soul must listen. The man in us is sometimes heard above the sinner.

So, too, God's yearnings may be held in check, for a time, in view of human sin. As it throws the soul out of a holy sympathy with God, so it puts God just as far out of sympathy with the unholy man. And yet the yearning is deathless; for it is the outcome of his eternal nature. From this impulse springs the purpose to rescue the soul from the dominion of sin. The cry of the prisoner and the craving of God look alike for some way of deliverance. Very true, if we keep in mind only the one fact that sin offends God, we shall not see either how man can pray or God hear him. That fact only in mind, God ought not to hear the prayer. Prayer will the rather be the rod that, rising above all else, draws down the lightnings of avenging displeasure. Indeed, it is the constant insistence of the Bible that God will not hear the sinner's prayer while he lives in sin. And equally true is it that hiding from God, as the Bible represents Adam as doing, is instinctive. The man can no more pray than God can hear. The promptings of the ethical are beat back by the whole force of the voluntary nature, which actually and always rules the personality.

Before the man can truly pray there must be the advent in him of a new spirit. And on the other hand, before God can give favorable answer there must be an ethical satisfaction for himself; a sufficient reason, before his own sense of what is just and right, for his new attitude toward this new suppliant. And equally to man's ethical nature there is call for satisfaction. Man needs atonement as well as God. Each severed factor needs to be made one again, the two separated personalities conjoined.

And here comes in on us the rising glory of divine intervention. It is rescue for the wrecked mariner. The vessel sinks; the mariner is transferred to the rescuing bark. The fact of rescue by intervention, when taken into one's mind and heart, opens to the man a wholly new kingdom—that of divine grace in the Gospel. And in this new Kingdom of God prayer now comes to be vastly other than it was in sinless Eden. It is far more than the natural breathing of human desire into the ear of God. This whole kingdom of grace, grounding itself indeed on the fact that prayer is an original instinct, and communion with God an old ethical craving, receives now a new direction and impetus; it has now a new atmosphere in which to live and breathe and have its being. It is now no more the old way of the Eden garden, but it is "the new and living way opened for us through Jesus Christ." For the idea of human rescue through divine redemption has in it, by especial divine ordination, a place for the peculiar prayer which these facts evoke. Prayer is to do a work along the whole line of the new kingdom, as men are to become intercessors on earth for others, in some sense matching the intercession that goes on in heaven. Human prayer is to be, in the new system, a grandly honored means of grace. It is called into a new position, clothed with new power, and given new scope in the new kingdom. And the man first is to be rescued himself, and then through prayer and those things that go naturally with it he is to touch other men savingly. And whether one considers the men to be rescued in all the multiplicity of their interests, or the whole divine arrangement for doing this thing, there comes out the fact of prayer made more prominent and its answer more assured. Its scope is grandly broadened, and its flight has larger range, and its wing is swifter and surer.

And in this new spiritual kingdom are a whole

series of facts that sustain the life of prayer. What material things are to these bodily senses, these things of God's kingdom are to the soul. In this sacred realm we have the Christ of God, human and divine; the Word of God, also human and divine; the Spirit of God, the indwelling of whom in the human soul evokes the spirit of prayer. The kingdom of God touches all our nature, renewing all the moral faculties, quickening and clearing the mental vision, and even furnishing further on, for our bodies, a "resurrection of life." It is a kingdom world-wide in its scope, throwing over all our political, social, and religious life its new radiance and filling all events with its new meanings. Life can never be the same narrow thing, with its dull round of common-place, to a man who has "seen the kingdom of God." The whole great world of human interests is lifted and glorified. The kingdom has place and use and consecration for all the interests of art and science and learning and law. Nothing is there untouched; and all it touches is ennobled thereby. It is the kingdom of kingdoms; and at every point of its multitudinous contact with human affairs its King ordains that prayer shall be offered. Its establishment on earth as a kingdom, and every step toward its magnificent dominion over the human race, are linked not more certainly with God's promise than with man's prayer. God and man are the factors, and the answering is interwoven with the asking. In the strange and startling scheme the action of God and man are made interdependent. The prophet of Israel represents God as determined to do a definite thing, and yet it is added that he "will be inquired of" in prayer to do it; and if the prayer be restrained, the thing will not be done. This interweaving of the divine and the human is the unsolved mystery of God's kingdom. But this at least is clear, that by the impulse of their new nature and of the Holy Spirit of God there is the ceaseless cry of God's redeemed millions, who are praying "Thy kingdom come"—a prayer from the range of which nothing can be hidden.

It were far too much to say that sin as a fact in the world calls out more prayer than sinlessness would have done. But surely the range of prayer in Eden was exceedingly narrow. Its themes were few. It might adore, and within a limited range might ask. It could bring thanksgiving, but it could hardly remain prayer long, for it would find itself engaged in praise. It would be just the instinctive worship of a pure soul. That were indeed most fit and beautiful. Who does not wish he had heard an Eden prayer, had himself offered the simple prayer of the sinless state? But how little of all the wide truth it must have had which now we are at liberty to use in our Christian prayer. Adam's prayer could have had no high fervor. It was never a man praying as for his life. It had no confession of sin, no plea for forgiveness, no trust in a Saviour, no cry for guidance when the way was dark, no struggle for victory in the battle with wrong, no thankfulness for the intervention of divine grace, no intercession for a world that needed rescue, no tears over a Redeemer's cross, no sweet asking for dear ones by Christ's permission and "in his name." But, on the other hand, exactly so far as our soul is restored to God by the Holy Spirit we get back all the best things in Adam's prayer of innocence, while we lose nothing that it is our own privilege to ask as disciples of Christ. There come hours in one's Christian praying when all the suppressed longings of years gain the freedom of prayer and the liberty of praise. Eden comes back in its primitive glory, the bondage for the hour is lifted, and the soul's native aspirations find vent in Christian worship. But our Christian facts are larger and more wonderful than those of Eden. Our world, with the second Adam, is a thousand-fold broader in manifestation of God than was that of Adam in his inexperienced innocency. The redemptive idea in the soul bursts naturally into grateful and adoring prayer. In the midst of the grandest arguments about Christian doctrine in the apostolic Epistles the writer interrupts himself with his own doxologies of mingled praise and prayer. There are devotional hours when the great Christian facts rise grandly on the soul.

> "I saw a vessel, which the waves did spare,
> Lie sadly stranded on a sandy beach
> Beyond the tide's kind reach;
> Within its murmur of lamenting speech
> Long she lay there,
> Until at length
> A mighty sea arose in all its strength
> And launched her lovingly.
> And thus, alas! our race
> Lay stranded on the beach of human sin
> And misery,
> Beyond all help, until God's glorious grace—
> A mighty tide,
> All crimson dyed—
> Swept grandly in
> And set us free."

In the presence of such facts prayer is less a duty than a joy. And the words "continue instant in prayer" are less the command of authority and more the privilege of affection. The redemptive facts are always opening anew to the praying man. The discoveries we make in religion are among its most delightful experiences. They tell of a botanist who had met with a rare and beautiful flower, that he fell on his knees, carefully examined its stalk and leaf and blossom, and then raising his eyes to heaven he devoutly thanked God that he had so adorned and enriched the earth. So a man has sometimes felt in the presence of a text of sacred Scripture as it has burst into blossom before his delighted vision. Some verse, like that in which Jesus tells of God's great love, has stirred the soul to its greatest depths. "God so loved the world that he gave his only-begotten Son, that whosoever believeth on him should not perish, but have eternal life." In view of such a text the whole spiritual nature has been roused, and devout thankfulness has found expression in prayer which is as natural as is breath. Nor is the ecstasy unwarranted by facts. A praying man has sometimes been obliged to stop in his prayer, and there, on his knees, assure himself by argument that it was all really true that God gave the Only-Begotten; and when recalling the certain historic fact, and the divine warrant for prayer, he has resumed his petition and gone on exultingly "in His name" to the reverent and tender and closing "Amen."

And Jesus Christ is not only the medium through whom we pray, but our example of prayer. His earthly life teaches us that even a perfect human soul must pray. The King in the kingdom of grace bows the knee and shows his followers how to offer their hopeful petition. So that prayer is for persons of highest moral grade as well as for others. It is the spontaneous act of the loftiest type of manhood. The better the man the stronger the impulse to pray. Our Lord is found, not only using hours in communion with God, but fortifying himself for wonderful deeds on busiest days by spending whole nights in prayer. On him as a man came the Holy Spirit. Even the associated divinity did not give him the kind of preparation needed for his peculiar mission. He must be like his people in this, that he is, while on earth, in that branch of the kingdom of God ruled over by the Spirit, whose work is especially to influence human souls and put them into the receptive mood toward the truth God has to reveal. Were we as pure as Christ we should still need a peculiar enduement of the Spirit of God to fit us for our place in the spiritual kingdom. And this blessing comes through prayer. Of our Lord it is said that "as he prayed the fashion of his countenance was altered." It was transformation by beholding. We too are changed in our prayer, "as by the Spirit of the Lord," so that we become anointed and appointed to offer up spiritual sacrifices acceptable to God.

But out of the closet, as well as in it, we are to pray. Set periods of devotion are not inconsistent with continuous prayerfulness. There is an insect which possesses, it is said, the power of surrounding itself with a globule of air within which it floats unwetted by any wave. And there is a devotional mood which sometimes abides for years, as God's special gift to a human soul. Then one is, as it were, ensphered in the moral calm, and undisturbed by any storm ever known on any sea.

Nor protection from evil only, but happy impulse along the lines of Christian activity; for never is there a path to tread, a load to lift, a work to do, that is not better done for this exercise of prayer. For the common labor and joy of life are connected with our spiritual career.

> "Hast thou within a care so deep
> It chases from thine eyelids sleep?
> To thy Redeemer take that care,
> And change anxiety to prayer.

> "Hast thou a hope with which thy heart
> Would almost feel it death to part?
> Entreat thy God that hope to crown,
> Or give thee strength to lay it down."

There is a natural relief to an overburdened soul in the act of prayer. It brings the burden and lays it down and leaves it. But God sees the act. What of his response? Is it not an answering act to our act in prayer? The answer is "abundantly above what we ask or think." God can no more be indifferent than he can be ignorant with respect to this prayerful mood of a human soul. And as he has a whole wide heaven of reserved blessing, we may believe that he will not fail to send out therefrom to such a soul some token of his remembrance.

The fact of human sin calls for peculiar providential dealing with man. And these providential events open fresh occasion on our part for supplication, and on God's part for the answer of intervention. It is a scheme in which all things can be made to work together for good to those that love God. Whatever may be true about penalty as necessary, even in providence, for bad men, it is sure that peculiar overrulings are alike the promise and performance of God in behalf of his people. Calamity has driven men to their knees. Trouble has extorted prayer, and the new and superior use of sorrow, not seen on the lower plane of even moral law, is shown on the higher plane of a gracious gospel. Evil has no tendency to righteousness, nor is it the object of penalty, as penalty, to do other than inflict deserved sorrow. But higher than this natural use of trouble is the overruling by which the divine chemistry of grace is shown. The trouble brings joy in the end; the sin opens the way to a possible salvation. Blind Bartimæus had been only a common Jew, with perhaps a special sneer for Christ on his lips, apart from his lifelong affliction. Had he been the favored child of wealth or learning, the question of personal bodily want, which held in it the germ of his spiritual want, would never have been so pressed on his notice. But he is blind. He is a beggar. His ear is quicker for the loss of his eye. He overhears the crowd talk of a miracle-worker. That is his need. All needs are akin. In his soul the man needs light as well as in his body. Jesus manages the interview so as to make the man pray. Then comes the answer of sight alike for the inner and outer eye. In such a probationary world there is the constant management of providence. God extorts prayer where he cannot persuade it. Life is now crowded with joys which are intended to evoke the grateful prayer of our favored hours; and now, again, life has its sorrows that press prayers from trembling lips, and we can only struggle toward saying, "Thy will be done."

Milton mourned his blindness in a sonnet which all the world knows by heart.

> "Seasons return, but not to me returns
> The sight of vernal bloom or summer rose,
> But cloud, instead, and ever-during dark
> Surround me, from the cheerful ways of men

> Cut off, and for the book of knowledge fair,
> Presented with a universal blank."

He, however, lived to regard his physical blindness as sent of God for the purpose of opening the eyes of his soul.

> "On my bended knee
> I recognize Thy purpose, clearly shown;
> My vision Thou hast dimmed that I may see Thyself, Thyself alone."

It is as true of our home life as of our personal that it abounds in providences that evoke prayer. How fit that the common joys and sorrows of the household should all be spread out before God; that the family devotion should pour itself out in entreaty for divine guidance in the days of perplexity and trial; that mercies, too, as they come and go, should be recounted at the altar of the home. In grief there is the prayer of submission; in joy, the thanksgiving of a happy heart. Burns' "Cotter's Saturday Night" has for its chief gem the stanza which describes the household worship, and Wordsworth finds homes of prayer amid the English hills.

Nor is public prayer to be overlooked. The instinct of worship, as universal as is the race, calls for its recognition in public services of devotion. Man's earliest recorded structure was an altar, and his most finished work on the planet, hitherto, has been the temple of religion. To deny this instinct its place, the sanctuary, and its time, the Sabbath, is to hinder if not to quench a human sentiment vital alike to civilization and religion. We read of a "place where prayer was wont to be made." Creatures of habit, we are to get wonted to times and places for exercise of devotion. And so closet prayer and family prayer and public prayer are all to be used by the man who would do his full duty to God and self and his fellow-man. For it is one's duty to others to do them all the good he can. And how can one do this except as he is in that moral mood in which he can supplicate God for all blessing in behalf of his fellows? It is as much one's duty to pray for men as to deal honestly with them; to give them an example in the matter of devotion as well as in every other line of human duty.

And so the range of prayer, widened by men's sinful necessities, is very great, and is growing in size as men see and feel the pressure of human want. And the volume of prayer is daily getting to be larger, since every rising and setting sun sees more men who are praying men. Says another, "There arises from all parts of the world at the morning and the evening, and through the labors of the day, a perpetual incense of adoration and of petition; it contains the sum of the deepest wants of the human race in its fears and hopes, its anguish and thankfulness; it is laden with sighs, with tears, with penitence, with faith, with submission; the broken heart, the bruised spirit, the stifled murmur, the ardent hope, the haunting fear, the mother's darling wish, the child's simple prayer—all the burdens of the soul, all wants and desires, nowhere else uttered, meet together in that sound of many voices which ascends into the ears of the Lord God of Hosts. And mingled with all these cravings and utterances is one other voice, one other prayer, their symphony, their melody, their accord—deeper than all these, tenderer than all these, mightier than all these—the tones of One who knows us better than we know ourselves, and who loves us better than we love ourselves, and who brings all these myriad fragile petitions with one prevalent intercession, purified by His own holiness and the hallowing power of his work." And these praying men, though all confessing to weakness and sin, give witness—and their witness is that of men who have no moral superiors on the planet —that God, for Christ's sake, has heard and does hear their petitions and send them answers; that answers are yet to come, since some of their petitions are reserved in those golden vials which contain "the prayers of the saints:" and, when the best time for the reserved answers shall come, they believe that these also shall be added to the great and greatly accumulating mass of testimony that God "is the rewarder of them that diligently seek him."

To quote from the many volumes of authentic and of personal witness, as to remarkable answer, is needless when every praying man testifies that along the lines of a vital and personal experience God has heard his supplication. Is there any other proverb so common and so confidently used in praying circles as this, that "praying breath was never spent in vain"?

CHAPTER V.

THE KINGDOM OF GOD AS RELATED TO PRAYER.

SPIRITUAL faculties are dominant by virtue of their nature. "The moral sense," says Mr. Darwin, "is the most important of all the differences between man and the lower animals."

Conscience is regal. It holds sceptre over everything done in any part of our complex nature. Considered then as a personal experience in a man's soul, "the kingdom of God within us" must use for its own purposes not only the soul itself, but the body and the mind as well.

In like manner, if we think of the "kingdom of God" as a world-wide reality, it must be regal. It can be nothing unless dominant. The final ends of all things must be moral ends. And the greatest of all realities, this moral "kingdom of God," may be expected to employ in its own advancement all mental and physical faculties. Natural laws do not work out of their own plane; but it is the mission of spiritual laws, *i. e.*, the laws of "the kingdom of God," to seek supremacy everywhere. Spiritual facts will then always be seeking to incarnate themselves in physical facts. Moral ideas will always tend to break through into their fit and visible expression. This is the true genesis of the creation. Natural facts are intended, more or less truly, to express spiritual ideas; they are more or less fitted to do it, and they are capable of being employed of God both in usual and unusual ways for his moral ends. There is thus room for providence and for grace, room for ordinary working and for extraordinary intervention. Things are worked in the interests of something higher than things.

"Science is classified knowledge." The writer of Genesis, an adept in both Egyptian and Hebrew lore, asserts the primal law for plant and bird and beast: it was to bring forth "after its kind." The recognition of laws of nature is thus as old as the record of natural fact, though the name "law," used in this sense, is modern. The more facts we know, and the more we know the laws of them, the closer we bring a personal God, not only to the physical world, but to the moral world as well. Law is method. And the divine method of steady working in nature and of steady obligation in the moral world of things induces "confidence" or "belief" or "trust," which, needed everywhere, culminates in the New Testament, with its specific demand of "faith in the

Lord Jesus Christ" as the vital condition of the spiritual life. And a very direct expression of this faith is through prayer; and hence the declaration "Whosoever shall call upon the name of the Lord shall be saved; for with the heart man believeth."

In marking the progress of this spiritual kingdom we shall see, first, that God uses times of great physical want to make men prayerful. We shall see, second, that he employs general laws in the processes of his kingdom—a fact awaking grateful prayer. And we shall also see, further on in the discussion, that at definite eras God has given the evidential miracle, in connection with prayer.

(1) The very wants and woes which come out of human sin have been pressed into use in extending God's kingdom. Sorrows are not blessings in themselves. Physical pain is not the award for right-doing. But by the wonderful overruling power of God those penalties which follow sin as shadow follows substance are made of spiritual use. Physical want has evoked prayer. Nature in agony is not atheistic. The soul's prayers are sometimes extorted from unwilling lips at the outset of a new life. Afflictions are used as God's angels. He compels recognition. The marshalling of events, now in the personal life

and again in the national history, has made men say, "That is the finger of God." Now and then the drapery falls off the arm, and God bares it, so that men see him interfering at the exact time with some remarkable providence which changes the fate of a nation. Then men are called to stand still and see the glory of God. Then the usual calm of indifference is broken and God speaks and all men listen. And a nation sometimes adds the reverent "Amen," while prayerful disciples lead a waiting host in their supplication or their thanksgiving.

It may be urged that such hours are hours of excitement. Granted. But why not here the excitements of noble feeling as elsewhere men yield to baser impulses? Such elevated hours are most honorable and the experience of them most trustworthy. We are made glad that our human nature is capable of such excitement. We are nearer in them to our normal state. The image of God shows then fairest in men. The deeper down goes the plummet in these deep-sea soundings, the more profound is the conviction it touches that man, in the essential nature in which God originally made him, was meant to pray and was a being made to receive divine answer. In our truest moments, when the great emergencies of being are on us, and we are stripped of the conventionalisms that clothe so much of our outer life, and we get back to our real selves and look upon our deeper wants, we find that we cannot do without a God to whom we may speak, and who will speak to us in turn.

And spiritual as well as physical want has drawn men to look away from self to God in prayer. In numberless cases men have sought God separately, and then have come out of the closet to find men all about them led in the same way. Men have prayed singly and then prayed in companies, and the place has seemed almost to be shaken; and even nations have shared in the impulse to call on God in times of broad and profound reformation. So that national distress has played its part in starting the soul's cry for its God. The dark days of personal and national life have been those in which the divine visitation has been especially sought. "In their affliction they will seek Me."

(2) God's use of *general laws* in the physical world has been in the interests of religion, and so has helped men's faith in prayer.

As to what are popularly called the "laws of nature," some strong thinkers contend that the phrase simply voices a conception that exists only in our own minds. It is, they claim, only a mere phrase that covers our ignorance; at most, that it is but our poor human method of conceiving God's way of doing things. A law of nature is our statement, they say, of God's ordinary procedure so far as known to us. So that a miracle would be his activity in unusual ways. Thus laws of nature, it is said, exist for us and not for Him.

But others claim that God's regularity in doing certain things can be nothing else or other than the result of a definite plan that he will so do them. And, thus, a law of nature would be the expression of his orderliness in acts. All hangs on his will or plan. It is even possible to conceive of the laws of nature as being very different. There was no necessity for creating at all; none for arranging these great general laws; none for this evolution by fixed laws working out a series of results. And careful scientists are pointing out the fact that as the physical universe, with its objects and the laws of them, began to be in time, so in time it and its laws will end; and they have it for a problem of actual calculation to discover when the physical energy will have expended itself. They are asking, What then, when this form of things shall have passed away? It is said that the system of general laws, admirable for many purposes, has such lack of adaptation to other ends as to show it to be a dispensation not always to endure. It was introduced to supersede a former system, and it will be abrogated in behalf of one that is to follow. And so it is claimed to be not impossible that Infinite Wisdom should put it aside at will, in the interests of the spiritual kingdom. We do not need to claim that any such suspension has ever occurred. Great enough to manage all physical laws in the interests of his kingdom, we may mark with delight God's method of holding himself to his fixed law, and yet so working events that, as a whole, they accomplish his final ends. The material system hangs on his will, is supported by his arm, and lasts as long as he shall choose. Here is the place for devout ascriptions of glory to him who formed this wide system of fixed physical law. All things are included in his plan. Let him be thanked. All his works praise him. No thoughtful man may be mute. We will magnify and laud his name. All orderly and beautiful things, all evolutions of his vast and comprehensive system as they come out into view, shall not only wake our delight but stir our devotion. It is for his honor and for our good that we daily perceive and acknowledge his method of ruling the world by law. So that this benignant aspect of nature shall be a source of our spiritual comfort in God. The bow of promise thrown across the retreating tempest-cloud, a thing occurring indeed under natural law, is ordained of God as a sort of natural sacrament. It is to be associated evermore in human history with the divine promise that seed-time and harvest shall not fail. The bow spanned an altar. And to primitive man there was taught the alphabet of that great literature which the more advanced centuries must learn, viz., that all physical things, seen with anointed eyes, are the visible symbols of spiritual facts. They are intended to stir the heart to prayer and the lip to praise.

(3) The kingdom of God has had eras calling for special intervention; and these have been times of especial movement in prayer.

So far as we know, there was no intervention upon the established order of nature for twenty-five hundred years. The primitive ages must learn to trust the stability of nature, and see in it token of the stability of God. But a lesson over-learned may be as injurious as one unlearned. The danger to the nations in Moses' time was not of non-belief, but of over-belief; not of thinking that God was not, but that there was nothing save God. From the stability of nature men have deduced Pantheism—the belief that God is all. And the opening words of Moses' story of creation are a protest against this misreading of the universe: "In the beginning, God." There was a personal being distinct from the world. "In the beginning God created." Then matter is not God, nor the universe an emanation from his substance, but simply a work of his hand. "In the beginning God created the heavens and the earth." Then the world is not eternal nor necessary, but a created fact in time, and standing in the will of the Creator. The historian, looking back from the days of the exodus, wrote as if a spectator of the genesis. He sees the creation of plant and bird and beast. He recognizes the law of "after its kind" as the method of development. Science started there, in the recognition of fixed general law. But religion started also in the same great Theistic fact. And the worship of the unchangeable Creator was the unchangeable duty clearly seen by man. Only this is to be noted: that the steady gaze of a man on this form of the fact has always the danger on the one side of falling off into the scepticism that says "law is enough without a personal God," or else, on the other side, into the pantheism which says "all is God." Universal materialism or universal spiritism were the two equal dangers of the world when Moses wrote his Genesis. The first would tend to atheistic denial, the second to pantheistic indifference. The latter was the tendency of Egyptian thought as felt by the Hebrews in

Goshen. And against it Moses would guard his people, and the whole wide world which should read the story of creation from his pen.

But the Hebrew was to find his trial in the monotony of fixed law. He longed for intervention during the dreary years of Egyptian bondage. There had been no notable interference with the regular routine of nature for centuries. If God did not come in some new way, then his promise would fail. The era at length dawned. The hour struck. The prayer was heard. The cry of the slave moved the arm of Jehovah. The cycle had come round. Creative power had intervened once on what was an older order, and saving power might intervene to keep the creative work from moral failure. Ruin stared them in the face. Salvation was the only hope from annihilation. The ever-present idea of a spiritual salvation bursts through into the realm of the physical; and supernatural deliverance is God's object lesson. The salvation of the people of Israel is to be a teaching for all time. It shall teach the world, as each individual looks, at some period of his life, upon the question of personal and spiritual salvation. Millions of men shall learn, each for himself, of God's spiritual intervention in the hour of the soul's struggle with the bondage of sin. We do not read this thing into the story; God put it there. His deeper thoughts are always striking through the shell of the outward world. There is a transparent dial on the watch-tower of human history, and God is the light behind that makes it an illuminated dial which gets the gaze of men in the darkest night. And the man who led his people to salvation, and through whom the deliverances at the Sea and in the Wilderness were wrought, was himself a praying man. He lived and walked and talked with God as a friend. In that march, more celebrated than any other in history, in which he led an undisciplined horde through unparalleled difficulties to a splendid success, at every turn he called on God. Next after our Lord's intercessory prayer for his disciples, the grandest instance of that kind of petition the world ever saw came from the heart and lip of this man Moses. Every miracle of his is born in prayer. He is clearly the greatest genius of his time, and yet in nothing more remarkable than in what, if one may reverently say it, may be called his genius for prayer. One of his odes—or shall we call it his prayer?—sounds down through the centuries, and is read to-day at the grave of our dead. "Lord, thou hast been our dwelling place in all generations" is still the funeral march of the world. Its tread is stately. Its music, touching widest extremes, has nowhere a false note. From the serene heaven where God sits from everlasting to everlasting in solemn enthronement, the song comes down to the earth and finds man in his three-score years and ten, and these years are labor and sorrow and he returns to the dust. And the organ tone is steady. The amazing transition has no jar. The song is sustained in all its variations. The man who made this song or offered this prayer had been much alone with God. He is priest as well as prince.

If we examine closely the miracles of the Deliverance, we shall find them so wrought as to put honor on natural laws. The Nile at times even now is red; but it is made to run actual blood. The lice and frogs at certain seasons are a natural plague; but they are made intolerable. Diseases of the skin, always the pest of Egypt, are made absolutely unendurable. First-born sons have died before; but a first-born child dead in every Egyptian and not one in a Hebrew home, on a given night, was a form of dealing about which neither stupidity nor perversity could possibly make a mistake. Not in one case was a law of nature repealed or even suspended. Just the opposite of that was what was done. The laws were used intensely, with greater energy. They were worked with supernatural might. Anything like suspension would have meant atheism to the Egyptian, would have made him cry out the rather, "There is no God." This intense working of law until it amounts to miracle is the thing that makes the Egyptian say, "There is a God; and that God is Jehovah." The whole transaction honored law and honored God. The great mark was set on those events, so that in all ages we can see the difference between the false and true miracle. The true sign from God uses law for all it is worth; it frequently obtains its results by infusing superior energy into natural law; while the false miracle has no basis in nature and no use for law. The "east wind" at the Red Sea has its place as well as the rod of Moses. The "few loaves" and the "small fishes" have a place in the feeding of the thousands. Miracle is always, in part, natural. It is never entirely outside of physical fact and law. If it were an outside thing, it would be only a "lying wonder." Its rank would be that of the "ghost story." True miracle is never without its material basis. God honors natural law in the Biblical miracles in every case.

The separation of Israel from Egypt, their transportation to the Sinaitic peninsula, their national organization, and their religious vitalization, are all miraculous in a peculiar result, never before sought and obtained. That new national and religious life is the miracle of history. For, starting there in that Arabian desert, there have gone forth to the world certain ideas of righteousness that differ, by the whole diameter of human thought, from any other ideas the older nations had ever known. Hints of the idea of righteousness, of the clear whiteness of the divine nature, the reality of holiness, had been given to wandering patriarch and scattered tribe. But they had died out of memory, if indeed they had ever been given into its charge.

Among these conceptions was the peculiar one of prayer to the Holy God through a Holy Propitiator. There had been unholy gods and unholy propitiations, unholy sacrifices and offerings for unholy ends. But this Hebrew idea was unlike any other the world had known. There had been, in these mistaken propitiations, the expression of a craving after God through some mediation. It was a blind instinct, and in that form working mischief. Now, for the first time on any large scale, the conception was to be rid of superstition, and the idea of a holy propitiation was to find its fit form. That whole Jewish ritual worship was simply a visible prayer. It was man, the separated, drawing near to God in a kind of literal and visible way. And the worshipper came always through a ceremonially clean bird or beast. The first offering, the smoke of which ascended each morning to heaven, was that of a lamb sacrificed—a lamb, the emblem of purity. But the lamb was slain—the emblem of purity making by its death, representatively, a propitiation for man the sinner. And the last sacrifice, when the sun was sinking into the Mediterranean, was the same offering of purity for sinfulness, that man might be accounted pure for the sake of the great Propitiator, whose coming was the fulfilment of the law and the hope of Israel and the salvation of the Gentiles. It was objective, tangible prayer. It was addressed to the eye of God. It was prayer done rather than uttered, made rather than said. It was God teaching man to pray by material things and by external objects. It was the use of the physical for the spiritual. It was indeed a form of primary instruction; but the foremost scholars of the moral world were still in the primary class, and they needed to be grounded in those terms of the moral alphabet in which was to be written the gospel literature for the ages to come.

In the march of Israel, when Sinai was left, we see the blending of law and miracle, and how both induced men to pray not only in the tabernacle but by the wayside.

Take the wonder of the manna. From Egypt to Canaan was forty years. During that time the scanty valleys about Mount Seir yielded only a meagre supply to the numerous host. Their food was supplemented by the descending manna, which seems to have formed in the night under the clear sky. It was claimed that it fell from heaven. Suppose a Hebrew, born twenty years before the Exodus. With devout heart in Egypt he learns to worship the God who is Creator and Sustainer of all things. The regularity of day and night, of seed-time and harvest, impresses him. God is manifestly to be depended upon in all the world; and the spectacle calls forth his daily thanksgiving. This man enters the desert with his people. He sees the manna every morning which had been deposited during the night. He recognizes the new wonder. It is a miracle from the hand of God for the support of Israel. God has intervened. This man is devoutly moved, prays with new gratitude, and begs that the miracle may be continued until the people can come to the land of promise.

Another Hebrew was born twenty years after the Exodus. Six days of the seven he sees, from his earliest childhood, the manna lying on the ground. It is the expected thing. It occurs regularly. He never has known anything else on six days of the week. He is no more astonished than is the boy on a New Jersey peach farm to see once a year peaches on the trees. It is nature. It is exactly such an event as might be expected. There is some sort of law that brings it about. It is no more miraculous than the sunrise. It is no more a sign of anything peculiar than are the starry skies. It is plain that what was miraculous to the one man was only common to the other. What then, is there no line between the natural and the miraculous? Yes; but it does not run along the line of what is more or less an exhibition of God's power. For, so far as we can see, it would take just as much power to have to-morrow's sun rise in the east as to have it hindered from rising. Nor does it depend upon the recognition of God's hand in one thing more than in another. For we are to see equally God's hand in the grain that waves in Egypt and the manna that falls in Arabia. Yet we call the one natural and the other miraculous. It is clear, then, that we cannot always draw the line at the time. The natural to the man born twenty years after the Exodus would be the supernatural to the man born twenty years before. But neither of them had the true perspective. They did not see God seeking one end in two widely different ways. They could not, as we can, take in the whole meaning of the era that called for the manna to come, and, equally, for it at a given point to cease. We are able to look back now and see that those forty years were the turning-point in the moral evolution of that race. Certain physical manifestations were demanded in order to accomplish moral ends. The miraculous is credible in its own time and incredible elsewhere. We, with wider vision than either of our two Hebrews, can praise the God who now by the regular course of nature, and anon by special intervention, was using nature for the moral advancement of his kingdom. Miracles he does not scatter promiscuously. They have their hour. They meet the crisis and depart. God can use them here, and use natural law in its ordinary workings there. They can never for a long time be common. And when we are asked whether God cannot at will break through the physical order and give miraculous answer to prayer, we must always reply in the affirmative. But when asked whether he does do it, and is to be expected daily to do it, we must answer by denial. Whether he will do it or not seems, judging by all past history, to depend upon the particular position occupied at the time by his advancing kingdom. He works by eras. He has his "set times." And when these eras come round again, it is reasonable to believe that he will not fail in the needed miracle. The ordinary and the extraordinary are both at his hand and stand waiting his use. Nor can we tell when he will use special intervention. At times we men, in our impatience, feel that God must speak out; that he cannot longer delay special manifestation; that the prevalent form of unbelief demands miraculous answer to prayer. How sometimes our human impatience must provoke the patience of God! Men say, Let there be at least semi-miraculous things done in answer to prayer. As if there were no answers if no miracles. As if we men knew "the times and seasons." As if we rather than he had notched the calendar of the ages. As if we could instruct the Omniscient One. The largest and longest opportunities for spiritual progress must come in between these eras of miracle. For it must be with emergencies as it is with miracles; they depend on their infrequency for their character. As all extremity would be no extremity, so all miracle would be no miracle.

And this is the reply that might be made to those who tell us that were there only faith enough in the church we should have miracles, at least in the form of bodily healing, on every day of the year. It is forgotten that in such a case the miracles would not be miracles at all.

Through their very commonness they would mean nothing as special intervention. In that case, let us remember that miracles would be most frequent when less needed. A very great measure of faith and prayerfulness might be able to dispense with them altogether. It is forgotten, too, by those who urge this view, that the Scriptures represent miracles as gifts of emergency, coming when faith in the great mass of God's people is low and prayer is slack on the part of good men. The undevoutest time in Hebrew history was the era of the miracles of the Exodus. Miracle is the resource of emergency. When Elijah's round of miracle came to the nation it was not because of the national prayer and faith, but the rather because of spiritual dearth. It was not the reward of great faith, but an incentive to it. And our Lord's miracles met an emergency when the national piety was at its lowest ebb. Miracle is interference for salvation; and its eras are when love is cold and faith is weak in the people at large and only a few are waiting on God. It is the hand of God's intervention thrust in to secure the attention of a slumbering world. It comes not in hours of abounding faith. Such hours can do without miracle. Those who believe most need miracle the least. It is intended to meet and counteract unbelief. An age of faith would be harmed by the distraction of too much physical manifestation. The time must be an evil time to call for such intervention in human history. A few must pray in the present position of God's kingdom; but the era as a whole will be lacking in prayer. And this lack is the emergency which makes the miracle possible and credible.

When Israel had established themselves in Canaan there went by the regularly ordered years. Fixed law ruled the times. At length came an era threatening the national life. God, ever present to the few praying men, seemed far away from the many. There was call for the advent of "the Prophets." They were cometary men in their mission. They were sudden in advent, rushing in from outside the regular order and work of the priesthood. They attracted attention by the abruptness with which they came and went. They speak and go. They are a "voice." They cry out. Looked for in the direction whence comes the cry, you do not see the man; you only hear words. It is a message left, but the messenger has gone. "Hear the word of the Lord," is the summons of the "voice." The aim was to startle a careless age. With them was miracle. It was the second great era, as the time of the Exodus had been the first. A few praying souls had wept and fasted and wrestled for a manifestation of God's hand. Oh, that "he would bow the heavens and come down!" And that was the very thing done in the cluster of prophetic miracles then exhibited to the nation. Those wonders told men of no new God, but only this: that the One who had wrought wonders in Egypt was still God. The former cycle had disclosed an unknown Jehovah to the proud nation on the Nile. The new wonders in Palestine were the manifestation of the well-known God among his own people. It was the distant God now made near, the absent God made present. It was the manifestation of a God vitally active and supreme. Idols should for once be counter-worked on their own plane. It was not a contest between a God and no God; but one which should show the true God superior to the powers of nature as represented by heathen worship. Elijah at Carmel took the idol prophets on their own ground. But no one can imagine that scene on Carmel apart from Elijah's prayer. The ascending prayer and the descending altar-flame are parts of one grand transaction.

Once more the ages go by. The nation again deteriorates. To a few waiting souls—"waiting for the consolation of Israel" is the happy phrase which describes their position—there comes the whispered secret of the nearness of the Messiah. He was born in the line of men royal in their prayers. His earthly mother was a praying maiden. His boyhood finds him in the " House of Prayer," hearing and asking questions, some of which may have been suggested by the visible prayer of the temple service. The new era dawns.

A Christ without miracles would be incredible, for he would not have met the world's want. But in the most stupendous miracle of his career, the raising of Lazarus, he offers the word of prayer in the same breath with the word of command. Sometimes, indeed, virtue went out of him mysteriously, though it were too much to say unconsciously. Sometimes the touch of the sacred hem of his garment was enough. But whenever there was need that men should specially recognize God, with the miracle went the prayer. When he left the earth, he left ringing on its air words which warrant the expectation that there were miracles waiting still to be done.

And here comes in a question up to which all these discussions on miracle and prayer steadily lead us. It is this: Do these promises of miracle hold good to-day? Were they for our time? or was there a restriction to apostolic days? Especially has it been claimed that "the healing of the sick" is a blessing granted for all time; that "the prayer of faith" can bring bodily healings which differ in nothing from those done by the Lord or the apostles. And when it is claimed that the days of miraculous answer to prayer are not past, and that only lack of earnest faith and fervent supplication is the hindrance to miracle, the matter needs to be gravely considered. For if it be God's will that "bodily healings" should still be granted on the plane of those in Christ's time, and if the fault is ours that thousands of the sick languish who might be healed and saved from death by our faith and prayer, there would seem to be a most frightful charge of inhumanity against us. Nor inhumanity alone; but we are holding back a demonstration of God's power which we were appointed to exhibit unto men. On the other hand, no innocency of intention can make it other than a most injurious mistake to expect, without warrant, a series of miracles to-day. The claims of wonderful results are indeed made. But, so far as can be ascertained, these alleged results are hardly miraculous. They scarcely exceed, if at all, those claimed by various specialists in the arts of wonderful cure. The advertised healings in the latter case are very numerous, and are often genuine. It is easy to use the word "miraculous" in a very loose and limited sense. But such a sense belittles the Biblical miracles and the moral truth that goes with them. A certain class of practitioners publish their cures, but not their failures. One can only know of the latter by learning of the single instances in local circles. There are religious circles where the cure by the prayer of faith, attempted by very devout souls, under the mistaken belief that miracles still remain, has not been a success, and in the terrible reaction a poor soul has lost all faith in prayer and in God for a time. To claim what God has not promised in the line of miracles is certainly dangerous. It may be as wrong to claim too much as to claim too little. It is not at all, here and now, a question about praying for the restoration of the sick as we pray for all other physical things that stand in any relation to our spiritual life. This is graciously permitted, and many know what it is to receive answers to prayer for physical things. But the question now is of miraculous works of healing on the plane of those in the days of our Lord. The allegation by some good men is that such things were promised, and that faith and prayer would bring them to-day.

The answer to these inquiries must depend upon the express words of the New Testament. These are to be interpreted by the laws which govern all language. They must be understood in their connection. And our idea of their meaning cannot but be affected by what we can learn of miracles in the past as pertaining, in their kind, to separate eras of the kingdom of God. The words will also be affected for us by the views which the study of the Bible has led us to form of miracles as *outside* evidences of religion, or as *parts of the scheme* of religion itself.

The verses are these:* "These signs shall follow them that believe. They shall (1) cast out devils; they shall (2) speak with new tongues; they shall (3) take up serpents; and (4) if they shall drink any deadly thing it shall not hurt them; they shall (5) lay hands on the sick and they shall recover." To these are added by our Lord elsewhere the words "heal the lepers," an act which comes under the class numbered (5). Also, they are (6) to "cast out devils;" and they are (7) to "raise the dead."†

On these passages, it should be noted that the air and tone of them suggest the local and the temporary. They sound like their age. Their color is that of the transient. There is no hint of their extension beyond a narrow period. They were certainly the things for that time; nor is there, as in other things that were to endure, any

---
* Mark, xvi. 17, 18. † Matt., x. 8.

hint of permanence. If they were to hold good during the centuries until Christ should come, it is more than strange that nothing is said about this kind of ministry as a permanent gift to Christians.

So, too, it is to be noticed that the words quoted from Matthew, viz.: "Heal the sick, cleanse the lepers, raise the dead, cast out devils," were given midway in our Lord's life, when the disciples were sent out on a temporary mission. The whole affair was local. They were not "to go to Samaria, nor to the Gentiles." It was a short preaching tour which they were to make, and they did not do even that. Their mission was a temporary expedient, and, except that they found "the demons subject to them," it was a failure; and this method of work was soon abandoned.

If it were true that the miraculous healing of the sick abides to-day, then, since the other gifts which are neither more nor less miraculous are named in the same sentence, the one class ought not to be exercised more than the others. Asked to "cast out devils" to-day, it is sometimes said that those "demoniacal possessions have ceased." But this is to own that one of the things commanded is local and is temporary. Asked to "raise the dead," which those disciples were told to do in the same breath in which they were told to "heal the sick," there is no other reply than that "Christians now have not faith enough to do it." But if it were a matter of faith, then the confession of its lack is most damaging to religion itself. An unbeliever has the right to say, "Raise a few dead men before you talk of saving any man's soul. For if your religion cannot do the outward and easier thing, do not urge us to trust it for the soul's salvation." By putting our holy religion in such a position we do it an unutterable wrong and damage. By insisting that prayer shall do to-day what it never was intended it should do to-day, by encouraging men to expect now those things which were indeed "signs" in their own age, we are injuring religion and are causing men to discredit the actual promises which belong to our own times. The reaction in many minds has been fearful. They have trusted promises that were not theirs, and in their disappointment have been spiritually paralyzed.

So, too, the emphasis put upon the miraculous healing of sickness has obscured the view of the spiritual blessings actually offered to us to-day. "Ye shall do greater works than these." But greater physical miracle than raising the dead is impossible. We are to see in miracles the physical scaffolding soon to be taken down, that the spiritual structure may be shown to the world. Moral results are to show "the power of God unto salvation;" and these are the superior gift —the sun that hides those stars. These are the moral miracles that displace, through the growing centuries, the crude but necessary displays of power in an era happily now gone by forever. Each era has its own kind of manifestation. The wonderful works which introduce it soon wane. Miracles come in cycles, serve their purpose, and depart. Some good men, who emphasize the Second Advent of the Lord, would see in "gifts of healing in answer to prayer" one of "the signs of the time" that the Lord's coming is near. But this is to mix strangely the peculiar "signs" of one era with the wholly unlike "signs" of another era. The "casting out of demons, the healing of the sick, the cleansing of the lepers, and the raising of the dead" are expressly said to be the "signs" afforded at the First Coming, while such unlike things as wonders among the nations and signs in the heavens will betoken the other. We do not look or pray for a repetition of the miracle at the Red Sea. It would have been incredible in Christ's time. It betokens, in its kind of miracle, its own peculiar era. No more may we hope and pray for the repetition of the

Bethany miracle. For the "raising of the dead" belonged to Christ's era, and not to the days of Moses nor to our day. The centuries do not go backward. The Red Sea is not to be divided again, nor Elijah's altar-fire be seen on Carmel, nor the sick miraculously healed, nor another dead man raised at Nain or at Bethany. We are past all that in our position in God's kingdom. We are looking for the "greater things than these" now, and awaiting another and very different class of miracles to come and close the dispensation. The field of right things for which to pray is so broad that we need not pray for the wrong things unto our own disappointment.

Just here comes into view a very important inquiry. Are miracles simply evidential, the *outside* confirmation? Or, on the other hand, are they *inside* the system and a part of it?

Very much depends on the answer. For if the first view is correct, then it would seem to be desirable that we should pray for as many as we can get.

The Roman Church has always held to miracles. It believes them continuous. It finds in them a token of God's constant favor to "the Church." It believes in them as special blessings to a holy person, or a holy thing or holy place. Hence nodding statues and sacred wells and healing charms blessed by church dignitaries. And if this be the true theory of the miracle, then its continuousness is one of the methods of converting the world. In this case prayer is to rise for them. They are to be asked for daily, and we are to get as many and as vast miracles done for the church as possible, thereby crushing out unbelief in the world. That would seem to be the first duty, on this view of the miracle.

But miracles, too frequent, cease to be evidential of anything special, and indeed cease to be miracles at all. On the Roman theory they are scattered over the whole dispensation, only with a growing frequency. There are to be more and more of them, and they are to be the fresh evidence granted to each age of a present God. It is forgotten that, even in the brief ministry of our Lord, miracles were so frequent as seriously to imperil the cause at one time. He must leave the crowd, or they would take him for a sacred magician. When his disciples came back from their preaching tour they showed themselves dazed by miracles. They cry out, "Lord, the devils are subject unto us!" But they say not one word about their preaching of the new gospel or its effect on men's souls. The cause was endangered by the constant demand for a "sign," which these disciples were so eager to exhibit.

Their hearers want wonder rather than truth, sign rather than salvation. If this was so because of the necessary prominence of miracle during the three brief years of Christ's ministry, what would be the result of eighteen centuries of growing frequency in miracle? Miracles were the needed authorization of the new dispensation. And they lingered awhile, the afterglow of the Lord's career. They did their work. They are still for our study. But as they slowly fade out before the better moral light of the established dispensation, we hear no apostolic voice praying for their continuance. Their work was done, and their glorious record remains to inspire us to pray for blessings now promised.

The other view regards miracles not so much as directly evidential, not as outside evidences of the system, but as an *inside* part of the system itself. They are indeed, incidentally, evidences. They are proofs, just as blessed and holy teachings are proofs. They come at eras, as the very overflow and outcome of God's manifestation of grace. They burst through and appear in visible form, as truth incarnate in fact, as part and parcel of the system. Their spiritual meaning is far more important than their physical form. They are great moral object-lessons. Historical facts they are, indeed; but they fill a moral niche.

Credible deeds they are, timed to a moral end. They minister not to credulity, as they would do if promiscuous in character and timed mainly by the will of praying men. But they come in groups and are gathered into eras. They cannot come out of due order. Moses' miracles cannot change places with those of Jesus. The kind of "sign" befits the kind of era. And thus while they minister to faith, they rebuke credulity. Studied in their moral aspect, as an actual *part of the moral system*, they have wonderful helpfulness in them. They mean more when they are past than when they were present. But they abate not one jot from their evidential power as parts of a system because their chief use is moral impression. They minister still, and with increasing force through the ages, to the spirit of prayer.

Nor does this view discourage prayer for physical blessings. Shall we pray for nothing save the miraculous? Are there no answers save miracles? True, the most answers will come in that spiritual realm of things where are our deepest needs and whence most prayers arise. But we are authorized to pray in hope for temporal blessings as they stand connected with the spiritual life and the Christian work. Mr. Muller has obtained financial answers. Hardly less remarkable are those given Mr. Spurgeon in the matter of his Orphan Houses. Hundreds of cases have been assembled in many volumes, like that of Dr. Patton on "Answers to Prayer," or Whittle's "Wonders of Prayer." Perhaps, however, more answers have been obtained to prayers for the cure of the sick than for any other class of physical blessings. And this not because of miraculous healings, nor a special ministry of healing for the body parallel with that of a ministry for the soul; but because the sick are many and the appeal to prayer for them is constant, and because there are especial promises thereon, which are not indeed in the line of miracle, but in that of plentiful blessing. Dr. Cullis, of Boston, records in his published volumes many cases of cure through prayer; and these cures, never miraculous, are often very remarkable. That he uses mental therapeutics on those who elect to be healed by prayer may be true. He instructs them to believe themselves cured; and it is certain that this "mental medicine" in all diseases is helpful, and in some diseases it is all that is needed. In case any wish to try the therapeutic power of drugs rather than mental therapeutics, he is understood not to refuse them. But in neither case is there anything inconsistent with asking and receiving God's blessing, in whichever one of the two methods the patient may elect. Mental and physical remedies are both open to us, and are to be used with prayer. And there is just as much answer when God blesses our wise means as when sometimes, in ways utterly beyond our knowledge, he turns aside the current of disease, and to the surprise of physicians the patient lives who they say ought to have died in the natural course of the sickness.

It is at this point in the discussion that we may consider the very striking words of the apostle James about the healing of the sick. The words are as follows: "Is any sick among you, let him call for the elders of the church, and let them pray over him, anointing him with oil in the name of the Lord; and the prayer of faith shall save the sick."

If these words be held to refer to actual miracle, they must be relegated to that time when "signs" of that sort were rapidly waning in the apostolic days. If miraculous, they belong to the introduction of the Christian era, and they were local in their application. But, happily, we do not need, by making them such, to put them so far away from our own times. Is there necessarily anything miraculous in them? Read them with the utmost care, and though they are peculiar, are they anything more than a large promise of abounding blessing in given cases? There is an absence in them of any one of the words the New Testament uses as equivalent to "miracle." Nor is the last clause, "shall save the sick," a more positive promise than many others from the lips of the Lord and his apostles. The only phrase which suggests anything peculiar is that which names the use of "oil." That phrase wanting, no one would have found in the verse the miraculous element. Excellent scholars see only the medicinal use of a single remedy. Others see here one remedy naming all the system of medicinal usage. Still others see in the presence of the elders and the solemn prayer and anointing a kind of mental healing. And it is not at all improbable that to drug and mental therapeutics there was also added the moral therapeutic of a profound religious impression. So that when all these means for body, mind, and soul were used, and there was prayer offered as the patient knew, by the whole church for him, he would be benefited, and God would add over and above all, his divine favor in the answer of an entire cure.* The passage then would teach us to

---

* In his "Notes on the Miracles," Trench, discussing the bodily healings wrought by our Lord, says: "He links his power to forms in use among men. It was not otherwise when he bade his disciples anoint with oil the sick. Without the oil—one of the most esteemed helps for healing in the East—the disciples might have found it too hard to believe in the power which they were

use all the means, and fail not also to pray in faith to God. So read, the passage agrees with that great class of Scriptural verses which cover all our wants; which bid us bring all our interests, personal and public, bodily and mental, social and political, to our God in earnest prayer. "Men ought always to pray." "Ask and it shall be given you."

And when we consider that sickness of body is so common, that its victim comes visibly nearer to the end of his probation, that it is often of immense importance to God's cause that a single life be prolonged, a given man be exempted for a time from death, we are moved upon by all these considerations to pray with earnestness and faith for healing mercies upon our sick. There are vast numbers of men now living who believe that along this line of prayer they have had God's answer.

When a peculiar era is on the world, and the progress of God's cause demands it, he has an Elijah who can shut and can open heaven, as the divine will may be. But when the physical shall

---

exerting, and those who through faith were to be healed, in the power which should heal them." Edersheim, in his charming volume on "Jewish Social Life in the Time of Our Lord," says, 'The means used were medical or else sympathetic or even magical. It was the custom to anoint the sick with a mixture of oil, wine, and water."

give glad place to the spiritual in the advancing cause, then the normal condition of daily spiritual answers shall resume its place. But Elijah's prayer on Carmel shall be all the more instructive because, instead of looking for a descending altar-fire, we are inspired to expect, on a vastly higher plane, the wonderful manifestations of a converting and consecrating Holy Spirit. And yet, whenever the physical shall stand in close relation to spiritual things, we will humbly but boldly ask for those temporal things which lie clearly within the range of our promises. And Elijah's example of fervent petition and God's answer on Carmel shall rouse us to believe that "the effectual fervent prayer of a righteous man availeth much."

CHAPTER VI.

PRAYER AS RELATED TO NATURAL LAW.

"How is prayer answered without violating natural law?" asks a friend.

Suppose we are not able to give the method. Suppose not one ray of light had been cast by all the investigations of six thousand years on the question of how God does this thing. The fact would not be disproved on that account. We should be on this matter just where we are about many another fact of God's universe, the existence of which is plain while the reason for it is hidden. Then, too, the greatest number of answers to prayer are purely spiritual, are in the realm of the moral and not of the physical world; so that they never touch the questions of material fact or force.

Nor is it needful, when the answers impinge on the physical realm, to think of them as necessarily "special providences," in the sense that they have no connection with that vast "general providence" by which God manages the world. For we are not at liberty to consider God as caring for some things and careless of others. *All his works praise him.* The distinction is not that some things are left to mechanism and others handed over to will and sovereignty. Considered with reference to a special thing a providence is special. It is God's care for atoms that gives him control of worlds.

But while the denial of prayer because its modus operandi is not understood is unreasonable, there are those whose faith has been confirmed by many considerations which thoughtful men have suggested.

It has been conceived by some strong thinkers that God, by the skilful use and the complete management of manifold combinations, can secure answers through known laws; so that by manipulations that are for the most part out of our sight he can obtain his results. Now and then the working of these laws, in less obscure instances, is held to give indication of what is always going on just beyond the line of our vision. But to make this the only or even the prominent way of the divine procedure, is to take a mechanical view of the matter. It would seem to narrow almost pitifully the range of God's working. It would introduce a kind of causal connection that scarcely leaves the divine mind liberty or discretion. It shuts him up as mere manager among his laws and forces, and conceives of him as exercising a kind of mathematical calculation in arriving at his ends. Not without some elements of truth, this view is felt to be too narrow to solve the problem. If indeed we were driven thereto, we might accept the theory, with the added view that the Omniscient God had provided for all from the outset; had so planned events as to secure by physical means all needed physical results; had made original arrangement in which he had foreseen the voluntary prayer and his own ordained answer, and had adjusted every law and assigned every force its due place; so that not otherwise than with infinite ease he works all things according to his will. And such a view must shut the mouth of every objector. And yet we are not so much concerned to remove difficulties as to discover, if possible, something of the method or methods God takes in gaining this result. There are many persons who, so far from feeling that the theory of management and combination of laws is derogatory to the Divine Being, see in that conception much that is honorable to him. Administration is genius among men. To stand with one's hand on the springs that move a nation is kingly. The old conception of God as far away, looking almost disdainfully upon the machine of the universe to see it run down, has gone forever. All who believe in any God to-day believe in him as near. The idea that God is not needed as one directly present amid the play of law and forces is an idea disputed by Carpenter, whose words in this matter deserve consideration. He says: "I deem it just as absurd and illogical to affirm that there is no place for a God in nature, originating and controlling its forces by his will, as it would be to assert that there is no place in man's body for his conscious mind." And he further urges that "the source of all power is mind." For God to be present and at work amid his own forces—for all forces are his—is to be where he can adjust and combine them. And not only by their harmony, but by the contact and even the clashing of antagonist forces, he can secure his ends. If in no other way, in this at least, he is present to hear and answer prayer.

And some have supposed a great hidden "law of miracle," and under it provision for answered prayer wherever miracle was needed. And as this cannot be disproved, if necessary, it may be assumed; exactly as our physicists assume the existence of the inter-stellar ether, the only argument for the existence of which is its alleged necessity. To many, however, the need for such a "law of miracles" is not apparent; nor yet the need, if there were such a law, of placing under it this matter of answered prayer. And yet to some it is helpful to think that in this, or in some similar way, God works out the great problem; and they are made glad in the belief that, either in this world or in that beyond, our sharper vision may at some distant period discern the principle by which, through the sweep of some law more vast than any we now know, God hears and answers prayer, even when the answer includes actual miracle.

And yet if we could find out the method of God, the thing discovered must be only secondary. And why need we spend ourselves on the question? If a new physical law is now, or at any coming time shall be, necessary, it can certainly be enacted. For are we not speaking of a God who has creative power? Bruce, in his "Miraculous Element in the Gospels," has well said: "We must hold ourselves open to the idea of a possible exertion of the Divine Will in the direction either of creation or of control, adding to nature's sum of being or disposing her forces to new effects." And this plea for miracle is equally a plea for prayer when miracle may be demanded in its answer. For say what we may about physical laws and forces, the spiritual beings in the universe are the greatest factors, and the way they are likely to act is the thing of far the most importance in our present inquiry. Laws wait always on executive volition. The force of gravity, as all other forces, is a minister in the hands of God. Personality is the mighty law. It rules, through God, all things. It is the basis, when we have said our all concerning other possible reasons, of our expectations as to prayer. Tyndall says, "It is a matter of experience that an earthly father listens to the requests of his children, and if they do not ask amiss takes pleasure in granting their requests. We know that this compliance extends to the alteration within certain limits of the current events of earth. It is no departure from the scientific method to place behind natural phenomena a Universal Father, who, in answer to the prayers of his children alters the currents of those phenomena." Not asserting it to be proved that such a Father is there, he admits that the conception is according to the "Scientific Method." This individual volition, this executive will in God and in man, disturbs not, so far as we can see, any existing laws. If needed, this could indeed be done. For God is their superior. Nor does law, at its last analysis, stand for anything save will. Fate and chance have no place in a universe that has in it a God. He, as an idea, excludes all thought of them. Law is a constant mode of divine volition. We see it in his plan. Plan never works itself. It is worked out by will. Indeed, there are those who conceive of all "laws of nature as immutable only in tendencies and not in results." Law is considered as always trying to fulfil its tendencies. But these tendencies are always to be used, as far as may be by man, and in a sovereign way by God. The illustration of the view is the tendency of water to run down hill. The tendency is immutable. But God throws a mountain in the way, and forms the lake; and the water does not run down hill. And man builds his reservoir and puts in his pumping machinery; and the result is that water runs up hill, its natural tendency not destroyed, but other laws are brought to bear, and so other results are obtained. No law is altered, none suspended. And this is a view not without worth as an answer to certain objections urged by those whose sole conception of law is that of mechanical, or some other form of physical, force. For law is not force, but is simply a mode of exerting the only force in the universe, the force of mind. Plan can be executed only by will.

And this leads up to that conception of the immanence of God in his universe which is just now attracting attention. It is simply the reviving of an ancient conception, and its investiture in modern garb. It is true that this doctrine of the divine immanence may be held in such a form as to differ in nothing from the old Pantheism. The extreme of the view holds men as "tid-bits of God." And all truth and error, all right and wrong, all things and beings, may be considered as having lost their separateness. They are bubbles on the sea of general being. Individual existences, at most, are considered as rising for a moment to the surface, to be resolved back into a kind of protoplasmic God. But any single conception of this kind, unmodified by related conceptions, runs into extravagance. Duly held, with its correlative doctrine of the divine personality, this idea is not only helpful, but it is explanatory. It opens a wide field of most interesting inquiry. It is the best antidote to the merely mechanical conception of law and force, and of God as standing among them rather than working in them. It certainly relieves many minds perplexed about prayer, and that too at some points where current views have failed to satisfy them. It is a view that accords with some very remarkable verses of the Scripture, which teach not only overruling, but indwelling. Another shall give us the doctrine. He says: "All the forces which control the physical universe, all the feelings which move in the moral and emotional world, are but the manifestation of the indwelling power of God; all the mysteries of the evening heavens, the relations of the material atoms and the unending miracles of organization of life, are only the utterance of the wisdom of God. Without him there is neither matter nor force, neither thought nor feeling, neither life nor organization. His presence is the essential existence of all things."* The conception is just, but it must not stand alone. "In him we live and move and have our being." "By him all things consist." But it is exactly as true that there is "One God who is *over* all," as well as "through all and *in* you all." Those who are pressing beyond its due bounds the doctrine of the immanence of God, are impatient of any words which describe God as working in any other way than *in* his universe. In their haste to make him immanent they make him impersonal. Immanence is only a part of the omnipresence which is as much *without* as within, as much *over* and above as in and through, as actual in superintendence as in indwelling. While avoiding the one error of a too mechanical theory, we must equally refrain from the narrowness which would destroy immanence itself by denying any other

---

*Roe, in "God Reigns."

method of the divine presence. We must hold firmly to an actual and objective universe, itself separate, in existence, from the God who created it once and sustains it ever. We must maintain our belief in fixed law, in impersonal forces, and in personal will. Says Le Compt in his "Evolution in Relation to Religious Thought:" "We are compelled to acknowledge an infinite and immanent Deity behind phenomena, but manifested to us on the outside as an all-persuasive energy. If we could understand the relation of physical phenomena to brain-changes, then we might hope to understand more perfectly than now the relation of God to nature." In such utterances there is no confusion of thought. For phenomena are approachable from within as well as from without. Mere physical science comes only in the latter way. A broader philosophy must take in the facts of mental science and of moral conviction. It must see that God stands related to all things, as man stands related to some things. The soul stands related to the body; so does the animal life—though they are not the body. Only we must be careful not to think of God as a mere all-pervading energy like gravitation. For the ever-present gravitation is due to his ever-present volition. The conception is still allowable whereby we say "God is a mathematician."

He looks *down* from heaven, and we look *up* to him. But he is a "God afar off as well as nigh at hand." "His eyes behold the children of men." And yet we are "temples of the Holy Ghost," and "God dwelleth in us." He created, and he remains in his creation. Sustenation is the successive throb of creative energy. When in prayer we ask him to "come," we are not more correct than when we own him "who is and was." It is not less spiritual to think of him as presiding *over* his works, nor is it less gross, as some would have it, to think of him as working *in* them. Control is as essential as abiding. How grandly, in one of his loftiest moments of poetic insight and spiritual feeling, does the Psalmist set forth his conception alike of the immanence and the superintendence of God, in the one hundred and thirty-ninth Psalm: "If I ascend into heaven, thou art there. If I make my bed in hell, behold thou art there." It is immanence. But he immediately adds, "Thy hand shall lead me, and thy right hand shall hold me." It is control from without. There are those who feel the difficulty of prayer when they consider law as fixed and universal. Equally would some be hampered in prayer did they think only of the immanence of God. To whom pray? To self, as "part and parcel of God?" Hold even rein over both conceptions, let them draw together, and prayer can be seen both as inspired of God and answered by him. He is nearer than we to ourselves. He is sovereign of law, and its vitality, as well. God is within all, behind all, before all, above all. He is executive as well as legislative and judicial power. We have to ask and seek and knock in prayer. Our mood and our need require it. And there must be one to whom this mood and need is correlated. But we are also to remember that God is in the closet before we come, is the sustaining energy of our souls while we pray, keeps up the beating of the heart and the coursing of the blood while we kneel, supplies, while we are at the exercise, the vigor to the mind as we think and the ardor of the soul while we feel. What should hinder, then, that he, while leaving us free, should influence the thought and the words and guide the petition toward the answer? We are not to think of him only as of a constantly equal presence, as is the air, but he is a person who is also spiritually nearer or more remote from our souls, who can "come" or "depart," who can give or withhold his favorable "presence" at will.

It is an altogether mechanical conception of the Holy Spirit of God to think of him as a constant volume of presence, and of our wish and will as the only thing that regulates the measure actually bestowed. He is not like the gas or the water furnished to your dwelling with just so much pressure to the inch, the amount received depending upon the angle to which you turn the thumb-screw of the burner or the faucet. It is not the even pressure of a constant quantity. That the Holy Spirit was historically given at a definite point in human history "when Pentecost was fully come," is a dispensational truth. Nor do we pray, in asking now for the Holy Spirit, that a certain period promised in the Old Testament may arrive. In that sense the Spirit has come. But in the sense of personal nearness we do rightly pray that he may come to men. "If ye then, being evil, know how to give good gifts unto your children, how much more shall your heavenly Father give his Holy Spirit to them that ask Him." "God is a Spirit." A spirit is defined as "a supernatural intelligence conceived of as apart from any physical organization." The Infinite Spirit is everywhere, working differently as now he creates and now he upholds the world; as here he frowns on sin and there he smiles on obedience; as he departs with his favor, though present with his notice, from the guilty, and as he fulfils to faithful souls the promise, "I will draw near unto you." The bearing of these views on the question of prayer as related to physical law is obvious. To many persons, some of these views are wonderfully helpful and even inspiring.

And yet we must always be on our guard, and make a sharp distinction between the fact and our theory of it. The fact of answered prayer would not be less credible if we were utterly unable to construct even a proximate theory of God's method. We can have a working theory, even as do those who speak of "gravity" and "inertia," which are assumptions explaining so many facts that they are almost considered as proven. What is called "chemical law" is in the same list. And the so-called "laws of life" are largely names for our generalization. We talk of the plant and of the animal life. But we have as yet no undisputed definition of life, and know nothing of what it is save that it is. The fact does not depend on the definition or on the theory of it. And if we could have no theory at all of prayer but had only the fact, that fact would stand fast as irrefragable. And yet, to see here and there, as in other things, glimpses and drawings of divine method, is to many persons not a little helpful when they come to pray.

CHAPTER VII.

NEGATIVE ANSWERS TO PRAYER.

A FEW years since, the praying men and women of this American nation were on their knees before God. The President of the United States had been wounded by a shot fired by a miscreant hand. As the long, hot weeks went by, the intercession of Christians for his recovery became more and more earnest. If ever supplication could avail, it would seem to be when,. from church and household, men of every party and every creed lifted up prayer that his life might be spared. Singularly enough, thousands of men, mistaking their eagerness for faith, made his recovery a kind of prayer test. Looking back now, those of us who passed through the trial of the weary days find that we had begun to think that there was in that case an opportunity for God to speak out, and the whole nation would own the fact that prayer was a power. We fondly hoped that for the strengthening of the godly and the confounding of the scoffer, he would do this thing. To us, the interests of religion seemed to demand that God should restore the loved President. But Garfield died; and the disappointed men who had prayed so long, at first felt that the prayer had been all in vain. Time has given us perspective; let us look and see whether there was lack of answer.

I. God's "*no*" is as really an answer as God's "*yes*." I deny my child; telling him that he cannot have what he asks. Is not that as much a reply as when I give him what he wants? Is not a negative answer an actual answer? Must God always say "Yes"? If so, we are the gods dictating to him, and he has dethroned himself in our behalf. How a child in your home shrieked when you took from his hand the razor he had seized; and how unkind he thought you that you did not grant him his wish to retain it. But you denied him, for the best reasons. He doubted your fatherly heart at first. But, child though he was, he never thought that your denial of his wish was the same thing as taking no notice of his request. God must have room to say "no;" and he must answer in that way a good many petitions.

II. In saying "no" to some prayers God answers them more wisely, not to say more fully. By denying the prayer of a nation for the suffering President, he taught us some truths this nation needed to consider. God's sovereignty, as we see it now, would have been put in peril in the minds of thousands, and the prayerfulness evoked would have never been so grand a moral exercise, but for those lingering, weary weeks.

III. We sometimes ask out of the line on which God is acting. It is now known that from the first the wound was fatal, and that an absolute miracle would have been needed to restore Garfield to health. It now transpires that the physicians, after the first ten days, knew that recovery was impossible. Medical science never has recorded an instance of a ball piercing that vertebra, in which the result was other than fatal. It turns out now that we were praying for a thing as unlikely—had we known what now we know—as if we had asked for a second sun to rise in the east.

But why did not God perform the miracle required and raise up the wounded President? To do so would have taken the world back 1800 years, to the last great miraculous era, when God wrought miracles on men's bodies. It would have been to turn back human history as an onward development of God's plan: to set back the world's moral progress for eighteen centuries. Was it worth his while to do that thing? Would any man, seeing what that miracle involved, have had God do that thing, even to save so precious a human life for a few years? The sufferer, had his paralysis allowed him to see all that it involved, would not have desired his life prolonged at such a price. Nor would we, knowing what now we know, though praying none the less for him, have asked that impóssible thing of a recovery. The ages must not retrograde. The kingdom goes forward to meet the new class of wonders yet to come, that shall suit the better time. As the burning bush of Moses and the descending altar flame of Elijah were the fit miracles in their age, but nothing like them could possibly occur in the New Testament day, so in our time, these wonders, in that grade in which the miraculous healing or even resurrection of Garfield might have occurred, are things of a past era. They are morally needless to-day. It was the peculiar stage of the kingdom of God that made them needful, credible, possible. They were epochal, not in Moses' time, but in Christ's time. In the one great epoch that remains, the old wonders are not to repeat themselves. The Mosaic miracles and those of the First Coming have each their specific character. The Second Coming is to be as distinctive. The eras do not repeat themselves in the evolution of God's thought.

IV. Nor was the praying necessarily uninspired by the Divine Spirit because the specific thing was not to be granted. God wants us to be practised in the using of our judgment. When in the "first commandment" we are taught to "love God with all the *mind*," the use of our *intelligent* nature is demanded. Mentality is to feed the flame of affection. Yet not a little of our mentality is wrongly developed, and must be always liable to error. Nevertheless, "the mind" is required, and it is "accepted according to what a man hath and not according to what he hath not." And praying for what, in its best judgment, a praying nation asked, its prayer was accepted as an act of devotion. Some prayers wait for years before they can get those answers which, when they come, are better than the things requested. John saw "golden vials filled with odors which are the prayers of the saints"—the unanswered petitions accepted as the requests of a piety that God holds precious. Who shall say what of protection from harm, or what of magnificent blessing lies waiting in the treasures of God, and is yet to be bestowed in answer to a nation's prayers? God has notched the calendar of his centuries, and keeps mete and measure of the ripest hours for the largest answers of accumulated blessing. And though, sometimes, before they call he hears, he may wait till a generation has gone before he brings the promised blessing to his Israel. When John Knox prayed "Give me Scotland or I die," it was a prayer that covered whole centuries; and answer still comes. When Judson had Burmah and Livingstone had Africa laid upon them as a burden, each praying for the country to which he gave his life, the prayer could not be answered in a day. The "golden vial" still has odor, and the prayer still rings in heaven, and the answer still comes as the years go by. There are prayers of long range, but the shot will strike the mark at length. Our prayers may go further than we think, as they may mean more than we realize when we ask. The near and specific thing involves so much this side of the possible answer that we think we are denied, though Omnipotence may be waiting on Omniscience to do the things that must precede and accompany the answer.

V. The answer has sometimes come in ways that we did not expect. We looked for sudden, almost miraculous, reply. And a far-off spring was touched, and another and a distant event occurred. We did not see at the time that the two were related, or that they had anything like answer to our prayer in them.

Never was more earnest petition than when

Jacob, fugitive from home through his own folly, vowed his vow, "If God will be with me and will keep me in the way I go, and will give me bread to eat and raiment to put on, so that I come again to my father's house in peace, then the Lord shall be my God and this stone that I have set up for a pillar shall be God's house." Twenty years had gone by. Every petition had been granted. The exact things he had asked had been bestowed. The exile had found a home, the starving one bread, the hunted man a relief from his furious brother. Back he had come to his father's house in peace. Flocks and herds abounded. Not a form of prosperity could be imagined that had not been given him. But it had all seemed to come so naturally that he had failed to mark the providential hand. Had some sudden fortune not half so large fallen from the skies, that would have been an answer to be noted. But flocks increasing year by year, and wealth coming in steadily from his fields, and the troops of friends always gathering about him, and the prosperity so continuous and through such natural avenues of increase, had seemed to him a matter of course and not an answer to his prayer. But there came a day when God reminded him of his overdue vow. And then it all flashed upon him. Not a thing had come, in all his fortunes, by chance; not an item of his wondrously changed circumstances but had been ordered by his God. And he woke to see that this was answered prayer. He hastens to Bethel to fulfil his solemn promise, and at every step he recalls the fact that God has signally blessed his ways. From another quarter than he had expected, the deliverance came. He had limited God; had fixed on the spot in the heavens which must be parted; but God had sent answers from the other side of the sky. How much that man lost by not watching for the mercies that had been falling on his path during every day of those prosperous years! How much more gladness, had he not mistaken nature for providence, or, rather, had he not forgotten that Providence uses nature in the answers of prayer! He had had for years that for which he was daily praying, and did not know it. And the answer he held to be negative was such only in his own failure to recognize its positive character and its gracious abundance. Perhaps it were neither unjust nor uncharitable to affirm that much which goes under the name of prayer is not prayer at all. A prayer of Sir Samuel Romelly is on record, as follows: "Almighty God. Creator of all things, Source of all wisdom, goodness, and virtue, and happiness, I bow down before Thee—

not to offer up prayers, for I dare not presume to think or hope that thy most just, unerring, and supreme will can in any degree be influenced by any supplication of mine; nor to pour forth praises and adorations, for I feel that I am unworthy to offer them; but in all humility and with a deep sense of my own insignificance to express the thanks of a happy and contented being for the innumerable benefits which he enjoys. . . . I cannot reflect on these things and not express my gratitude to Thee, O God, from whom all this good has flowed." The prayer from which this is taken is, every sentence of it, in exactly the tone of that here quoted. And the question occurs at once, "Is this prayer?" The author of it says that he does "*not* offer up prayers." What then does he do? He recounts blessings, and says he "expresses thanks," but immediately adds that he does not pray "to pour forth praises." He uses humble words, calls himself "unworthy," and calls God "source of all virtue and wisdom and happiness," and yet says he "does not pour forth adorations." Again we ask, what does he do? The prayer asks nothing; not even its own acceptance as a prayer. It is simply an "expression," as he himself calls it. It is an utterance of self-relief, an expression of gratitude that does not even ask permission to "offer praises" to the

One from whom these things that stir the heart do come. Its drift is toward thankfulness. But it insists upon not offering "praises." Yet why a man should deprecate "praises" and then "express thankfulness," except in hope that God would hear the expression of it, one cannot well see. If God can hear the thankfulness, then he can hear the "adorations," also the "prayers," also the "praises"—certainly the one as well as the other. The prayer looks like a studied attempt to do the thing and yet not to do it; to attempt to give vent to a natural impulse of fitness and gratitude; but the good impulse is beaten back by the bad theory, which is most inconsistently applied. He is uttering a monologue, which, though addressed to God, ought not to be, on his wrong theory of prayer. It will not be unjust, if we take the genial man at his word, and decline to call his "vocal musings" by the name of prayer. Let us hope, however, that inconsistent enough to address a prayer to "Almighty God," which he calls "not the offering of prayer," his heart got the better of his mistaken theory in the end, and that he came to God at length in prayer and praise and petition, all of them sweetened with his humility and gratitude.

VI. So, too, prayer may not yet, in a given case, have got on beyond that general sense of fitness and proper respectfulness in which so many stop. Men say "I hope and pray" that this or that may be granted. Some use words of opening and closing prayer much as one would write "Dear Sir" at the opening, and "Yours truly" at the close of a letter. The invocation and the closing ascription are the customary and decorous forms, to be as carefully employed as is any other formula of good breeding and polite address. We would not have men less careful for proper forms in which to open or close their prayers, especially when leading the devotion of others. But the devotional is more than the decorous, and prayer is more than the direction of an epistle. And there must be something between the opening words and the conclusion. The petition should not be omitted from the prayer. What would be thought of a petition that petitions for nothing? He who addresses a letter "To the President, Executive Mansion," and signs his name to the letter at the close, but inserts nothing of moment between, is a trifler. He cannot be said to ask anything of the President. Blank petition is next kin to blank prayer. Forms are well, though many a petition that was not in due form has received consideration from the Executive of the Nation. Even if a man who contents himself with a few moments of such prayer morning and evening, may satisfy thereby an easy conscience, he cannot hope to obtain an actual answer to a petitionless prayer. One should not indeed fail to "enter the closet," as the Lord commanded; but we should fill up the form with the fit words from an earnest heart. John Quincy Adams could say that never had he laid down at night without repeating the child's prayer his mother taught him, "Now I lay me down to sleep." Hundreds repeat regularly, at the bedside every night, the Lord's Prayer. Better the form of words than nothing. For, by-and-by, when there are inward movings toward real prayer, the strangeness felt by those who never kneel before their Maker will not be experienced. Accustomed to use the language, they will not be affrighted at the exercise. And then, too, the form of fit words may catch and grapple with the genuine feeling, and the body of the prayer come to throb with actual life.

It must be confessed also that some good men, afraid of forms, allow to themselves a kind of rambling in prayer which they would never employ elsewhere. Word suggests word, and the prayer is without form and void. An address to man, as inconsequential, as incoherent, would be absurd. Such a prayer written out would amaze the man who offers it. A letter to a friend would have at least some general order. A conversation in a parlor or by the wayside, would have some one theme pursued to its close before another topic was named. Shall we permit ourselves, in this miscellaneous address to God, rambling repetitions, sentences without connection, words used because we have heard them employed statedly in family or public prayer, with pauses in which one stops to think what next is to be said and fills up the gap by using some one of the many names of God,—are these the prayers that can claim answers? Persons unused to the exercise are not indeed to be criticised unduly. The heart may be full when the vocabulary is scant. And a young Christian is to be encouraged to pray with others as well as in the closet. But when years have gone by, a Christian, leading the devotions of his brethren, should school himself to orderliness and method and precision in prayer. Why not a Christian minister as careful about the public extemporaneous prayer as about his sermon? Why not a solemn recalling, before a word is uttered, of the theme, the material, the adoration, the petition of his prayer? For what is he to ask? If for more things than one, let him seek that they have orderly presentation, not only for his own mental and moral helpfulness in the exercise, but that his hearers may follow the order of his thought without distraction to their devotion. And, above all, the God to whom he speaks is the God of order. God knows and accepts us in our act of seeking out fit words, and mental as well as moral orderliness of thought and feeling, when we approach Him. For prayer is not a spasm of excited feeling that is careless of all words,—except indeed under those sudden occurrences when there is no time for thought. Then the cry of agony, or the appeal for help, bursts forth. "Lord save or I perish" is the cry of the sinking disciple. But the prayer of the closet, of the household or the sanctuary, is to be thoughtful as well as earnest, careful as well as devout, orderly as well as hearty. There is to be simplicity rather than that incoherence and overflow of stilted phrase sometimes heard. We are not to fling separate sentences at God as men discharge missiles into the air. And we cannot wonder that such petitions, so aimless and scattering, do not bring answers. When the man is more in earnest the prayer will be direct and specific: and then the suppliant may find that the answers which had seemed to be denied are really bestowed, and the apparent refusal is reversed.

And the prayer may wait an answer until it becomes a genuinely Christian prayer. Prayer in the case of a man who has known little about Christ may be accepted. Many a devout Jew has been so situated in life that the proof of Christ as the Messiah has never come fairly before him. In such cases acceptance may have been had through the Christ who was unrevealed to the soul. Says another, "The northern Aurora lights our midnight skies with scintillations emanating from magnetic vortices whose locality is unknown to us. So we can conceive of faith in a mercy without a known atonement and prayer without a revealed Saviour, as looming up in the radiant twilight to the eye of a heathen seer, because of the secret history of such prayer in its movement among the mediatorial councils of God." (Phelps' "Still Hour.") But for men of intelligence, living in this nineteenth Christian century, prayer that omits to take Christ as the way of access to God can only do so in express neglect of his own words, "No man cometh to the Father but by me." Prayer has one avenue to the heart and heaven of God. Not now to discuss the relation of atonement to prayer, it may suffice to say that if the original right to pray is gone through sin, and if the original instinct of prayer is beaten back and overpowered by the stronger heart, the "new and living way" of access is the permitted, if not the necessary way. To refuse it would be a slight and an offence. A guilty conscience craves a way for acceptance before an offended God; a weak soul craves another's strength, an overpowering sense of one's unworthiness craves some other name that is worthy, as a plea. "Of what are you thinking; for you seem lost in thought, this morning?" "I was thinking," said the carter to the merchant who had spoken so kindly to him, "that if I was only able, I would buy that cargo," pointing to a vessel just ready to discharge her freight. "What would you do with it?" "Sell it for enough advance to clear off the mortgage on my little home." "Go and bid it off." "But they won't listen to my bid." "Tell them you bid in my name, and here is a check to bind the bargain." At first as he bid, no notice was taken of him. By-and-by, he made a bid, and shouted loud enough for all to hear, "I bid in the name of ——;" and he mentioned the name of the great merchant. It was enough. The cargo was his. So we are permitted to come "in his name." It is a Christian privilege to name a name always heard by the Father. If nature shuts the door, grace in Jesus Christ opens it anew with a plea never refused. The Christian theory of prayer is perfect, and the Christian practice of it is warranted. And yet a man whose creed is right, may have overlooked in feeling, and omitted in practice, the privilege of asking "in Christ's name." And the answer may be withheld until, presenting in our faith the great plea, we gain, through Christ, a Christian acceptance.

And the deferred answer may be connected with our failure to take in the related truths involved in prayer. If Cicero might say that there is no knowledge that is not of use to the orator, then we may say also, that there is no knowledge of religious truth that is not of use to the praying man. And God may hold off the response until we take up the truth that is unused and yet so near at hand. If the Bible is the World's Prayer Book, not only in its formulas and examples, but also in its promises and in the truths it gives us, all of which minister to our devotion, then can God do a more kindly service than by refraining to give what we ask, until we make use of his Word in securing what may be called the material of prayer? He may wish to incite diligence in discovering truth. Made to wait, we may be led to ask why the answer delays, and so may come to seek in the Scriptures the larger truth.

And when one more thing is added, the series of reasons for deferred answer may be deemed sufficiently long. "Ye ask and receive not, because ye ask amiss." The remissness named by the apostle is lack of *spiritual* desire. The prayer must wait for its answer until some wrong is taken out of the way. The wrong feeling toward a brother man, the quarrel the bitterness of which remains, the transaction which we are not willing to review calmly because afraid we may have to say that there is sin in it, the plea whereby we justify conformity to the world—are all to be considered when we stand waiting for the answer that does not come. We are made to ask whether the cause is not in something we have done or not done. It will not take a large sin. A small bit of iron will disturb the magnetic needle. A small grain of sand will grate harshly in the delicate mechanism of the eye. The sin may be one so long petted and excused that we hardly see it as a sin at all. It may have woven itself into all the fabric of our social, and our business, and even our religious, life. A praying man, finding "dryness in prayer," should stop and ask for the reason. It will not do to say that one cannot always expect to feel in the same mood in religious exercises; nor to attribute one's weakness in prayer to God's arbitrary "shutting up of the heavens." It were better to reserve those for final reasons, if after having examined ourselves honestly there is found no reason within our own souls, or in the practices of our own lives. As Faber sings,

> "Oh, for the times when on my heart
>   Long prayer hath never palled;
> Times when the ready thought of God
>   Would come when it was called.
>
> "What can have locked these fountains up,
>   Those visures what hath stayed,
> What sudden act hath thus transformed
>   My sunshine into shade?
>
> "One thing alone, dear Lord, I dread:
>   To have a secret spot
> That separates my soul from Thee,
>   And yet to know it not.
>
> "If it hath been a sin of mine,
>   Then show that sin to me,
> Not to get back that sweetness lost,
>   But to make peace with Thee."

Baffled in life, prayer returning with shorn wings to the place whence it began, access denied, comfort departed, the man is thrown back upon inquiry. And there may come to him the words "if I regard iniquity in my heart the Lord will not hear me." The sin put away, the prayer can proceed. And the number of instances in which this experience of delay has been of use to a man, almost justifies the paradox of saying that the delayed answer is the quickest possible response of God.

Is it then so hard to get answers? By no

means. What one thing now named as a wrong, would we have God overlook? To the simple sincere soul, putting away sin and seeking all righteousness, willing to serve and busy in all duty, is prayer hard? Is there the forbidding bar? No, no, cry thousands. The way is opened into the Holy Place. They have fellowship, in prayer, with God. And some of them who spoke once of answers withheld, now bear witness that deferred answer is not denied prayer.

CHAPTER VIII.

REACTIONS LEADING TO PRAYER.

PROMISE is not always and only verbal. When the storms of a dreary winter have spent themselves, men are wont to find in the softer airs of spring as they sweep over the earth, the promise of better things.

> " Spring's real glory lies not in the meaning,
> Gracious though it be, of her blue hours;
> But it is hidden in her tender leaning
> To summer's richer wealth of flowers."

Promise is sometimes given to meet the instinctive reaction from unbelief, mistrust, and despondency. There are hours of depression, in which Shakespeare can write no play and Milton no poem. Into every life there come rainy days. Things go wrong. The world drifts and the skies are far off. It is even worse when, through erroneous views of life and destiny, a man loses hope. How easy then to misread all history! Herod wears the purple and Christ hangs on a cross. The pendulum stays on the other side of the arc. Nothing is sure but ill, and that is not an absolute certainty. There is no faith, but only dead negation; and the hands made to reach out to others and to be open upward to God, hang listlessly at one's side.' If this continues life is not worth living. Pessimism is death to hopeful view and earnest action. And God lets sometimes a man and sometimes an age work its way by storm into the smoother seas beyond. Only by reaction can some men and some centuries be reformed. For men, seeing where hopelessness leads them, start back. The lightning flash does not create, it only discloses the danger. In those reactionary moments a life without positive faith is seen as a mistake, and men rouse themselves to ask whether there is not somewhere a promise to which hope can attach itself; something positive, instead of those old negations. For we men are made to believe. Doubt is left-handed and goes off in wrong ways. The capacity for faith has its correlative in truth on which faith can rest. No man, no age ever made progresses by doubt, except as doubt led to the reaction of faith. Doubt never made a discovery of worth to the world. Never by doubt was the domain of knowledge widened by a hair's breadth. God gave us, as our greatest capacity, the power of believing on testimony. It is not what we are in capacity of natural powers that forms the limit of either our efficiency or our responsibility. It is our power of going out of self and receiving alike knowledge and potency from God—in one word, our *aptitude for faith*—that gives us our dignity as men. It is not so much what we have as what we borrow when the lender is God, that makes us of worth as men. The foot, made to "go," as if we were not where we should be—made to go to another—is a typical fact. And equally so, the hand, made to be uplifted and reached out, as if it had not what it wanted, and must take it as a descending gift from God above us—our hand receiving from His hand—is, equally, a typical fact. We must enlarge our schedule of man's powers, and add to his power of reasoning and to his power of imagining, the power of believing. We have been prosecuting, as an age, our religious inquiries mainly by reason. We must see our mistake in the resulting disquietude. And as clearly must we see that our success will come along the line of faith—a mightier force, as toward God, than reason.

God leads sometimes by reactions. It is to be noticed that a reaction has begun from the agnosticism so prevalent a few years since. Nowhere, except in the semireligious speculations of a limited class of scientists, does the agnostic creed "we do not know," have any place. It is the boast of the century that we do know, so positively, and about so many things. Why in one department alone so reluctant to be positive? Why not, as men are shouting out their joy over scientific truth—not indeed seen to be absolutely demonstrated in nature, but only shown to be necessary—why not the same exultation here? The atomic theory, the nebular theory of the worlds, the theory of an interstellar ether, the principle of gravitation, are all inferential. No man dares say they are proven. Yet no man says before them the agnostic words "we do not know," or the pessimistic words "we cannot know," and "it is all in vain to know, even if we could." We have had the phrases "Inscrutable Power," "Power that makes for righteousness," "Unknowable Power" and others of like import. Is it not strange that the word "God" is avoided, and that, too, when Tyndall says it is "scientific method to place behind natural phenomena a Universal Father"? But the reaction from all this is making itself felt. Frederic Harrison, not indeed in the interests of Christianity, as yet, but in that of fair thought, insists that the negation of religion in scientific statement is unwise, and is unphilosophical as well. He says "the net result of the whole negative attack on the

Gospel has perhaps been to deepen the moral hold of Christianity on society." He claims that "men turn from this negative attack with weariness and disgust." He insists that the phrase used by Mr. Spencer is "obviously only the flourish of a man who has nothing to say and who wishes to say something." Mr. Harrison's so-called "worship of humanity" is far enough from the full demand of his own premises, but to *worship something* is better than nothing. He insists that the agnostics must contrive some kind of faith, the pessimists get hold of some sort of hope, or retire from an attempt to lead the thought of the ages. The great human heart is in earnest. The trifling, scoffing, contemptuous mood has had its day. Religion is no more to be pitied. It, in turn, has pity to give to men whose cherishing of agnostic tendencies is coming to be seen, even by themselves, as mistaken leadership in an age, on the banners of which, in every army, alike of philosophic thought and religious insight, are inscribed the words, "this is the victory that overcometh—even your faith."

When it is once recognized, as it is sure to be, that faith is an instrument of human progress having its place beside reason, then pessimism will be dethroned and agnosticism be no longer the strange boast of men who exalt human knowledge. It will be seen that as the most of our alleged laws and forces of nature are not quite logically proven, but are believed in because it is logically necessary to hold to them, so in religion, when reason has done her utmost, there is room for believing in what a moral necessity compels us to insist upon as truth. Then comes the question of "to what staple the last link of this chain is fastened." Intellectual and moral necessity require a God and an immortality. Made to believe, there is some one to be believed. The one to be believed must have uttered some word of promise. Hence that name "the Word." He is the incarnate Promise. We are made to trust, and he is the one to be trusted. He who made all the links of the chain has fastened it to the staple.

Here come into the discussion the manifold verbal promises of the Bible. Had we but one of them it were an inestimable treasure. What of the "unsearchable riches"? What of promises for every hour and every occasion? Quoting is impossible. The whole volume is fitly called "the Word of Promise." It is one great appeal to men, who in view of it "ought always to pray."

Is there coming a reaction in which the thought of the age shall not only recognize the Father, but shall be also prayerful? It is instructive to note

God's methods in the past. A fact or doctrine in religion had fallen into desuetude. By a kind of moral reaction God has brought it forward again, and it has been so thoroughly fixed in the Christian consciousness that it can never wane in its brightness. Such was the case with the doctrine of "Justification by Faith" which had fallen into the background. There came a mighty reaction. For men's hearts needed an assurance as to their spiritual standing; and to wait for justification until the close of life or until the final judgment, was to consign men to a kind of spiritual bondage that ministered always to fear. The reaction changed all this; and men took in the fact that when we believe we are completely justified. The great truth filled Germany with song, and all northern Europe added its voice to the swelling chorus that welcomed the era of a believing Church. So, too, afterward, when religion had become a formality in England, there came the reaction, under the lead of Whitfield and Wesley; and religion as a personal experience stood forth before the world. It was claimed that a man should know that he had "passed from death to life," and the inward "witness of the Spirit" was declared to be the privilege of every believer. It was the era of experimental religion. It has been claimed that there has been likewise a missionary era; God bringing in upon men a new sense of responsibility to give the Gospel to the world. Is there to come also a *praying* era? Is it to dawn on men that praying for men is as much a duty as the giving of money for their necessities; that the other philanthropies that dignify and adorn our century are to have an addition to their force and number, by a newly used instrumentality, that of prayer? For, a force at all, it must be of no mean rank among those whereby men are to be moved for the better. Praying for men is equally a duty with the setting before them an example of honesty, sobriety, and of every religious virtue. Praying for men is a debt due them, to be paid like any other obligation. And when one reads the glowing words of the grand old trumpet-tongued prophets, about prayer being made among all nations, when one hears them declare that God will pour out on the nations the "spirit of grace and supplication," is not one warranted in the belief that, at some time, all human thought shall turn toward God, and that in the very desolateness of prayerlessness, men shall be ready for the grand reaction whereby the world shall stretch forth its waiting hands of supplication toward heaven. At some time there must come an age of prayer.

And as human thought, through the reaction born of its necessity, must seek God at length, so each soul must seek God by way of rebound.

It were indeed a more beautiful theory that each man, drawn by an inward and natural affinity and affection, should turn to God, as spontaneously as he breathes. Would it were so. But we are compelled to acknowledge a strange reluctance to go beyond a bare recognition of God. Nor is the fact that the logical compulsion of the intellect toward Him is overbalanced by the reluctance of the heart, to be denied because it is so sad and unfortunate a thing. And yet here comes in the reaction. The prodigal is a king's son in the far-off land. He begins to be in want. Forbidden to eat even the swine's food, half naked, sore of foot, and sorer in heart, he recalls the old home. Bread enough there, while he is perishing with hunger. In thousands of hearts there is a sense of coming to one's self, as though one had been under a sad spell of some evil power. The moral nature asserts itself. There is in every man a sort of race memory. No man can distinctly recall Eden; but there is a kind of dim far-away impression of better days for the race—days that were left long, long ago. They tell of a Russian prince, that he had been in early childhood spirited away from his home and brought up among rude fishermen. But always there was a difference between him and the fishers' boys; always a dim half-conscious memory as of a better condition and other surroundings. The human soul experiences this sense of strangeness, of absence, of degradation, of yearning for the Father's heart and home. It evokes prayer. "Father, I have sinned," bursts out from a pent-up heart. Nature in deep spiritual trouble is not atheistic. It knows there is a God. It turns to his Word. The key fits the lock. The promise meets the prodigal state. The Father meets the wanderer when a great way off; and they go back together—that forgiving father and that forgiven son—to the old home. The son had proposed to ask a servant's place, and begins to pray for it; but before he could get so far on in his prayer as to say "make me as thy hired servant," he is interrupted by the Father's call for robe and ring. There is to be no service of years as a menial. He is received in the palace as a son. The prayer of his subsequent gratitude is not given. Perhaps no words could express it. But we may be sure that the "prayer that differs in nothing from praise" was offered and accepted.

So too, by parallel experiences on other lines, God has wrought on men by these great reactions of the moral nature. Not that wickedness is preparation for godliness, but that its results in this world wake reflection. And a man who has stood face to face with ruin has reasoned back to the fact of his sin, and then has prayed for forgiveness. What is termed "conversion" is often reaction divinely directed. The conscience and reason and the soul itself, its native wants laid bare, cry out for God. Such a man has sometimes seemed to be on an eminence and looking down, by an intellect keenly alive, upon his soul spiritually dead. It became an agony that there was no stir of right feeling. He was convicted of not being convicted as he should have been. There is a strange contradictory deadness, of which a man is yet conscious. The soul, alert enough elsewhere, is unresponsive to divine call, and unmoved except as with a dull ache that is hardly a pain, at its spiritual condition. The very desperateness of a man whose nature will not vibrate at all to the touch of God, evokes a cry of anguish. It is the returning sense of pain in a body that has been bitten by the frost, and numbness is giving way to sensibility. It is the first promise of life. It is proof that deadness has not gone on so far as to death. And when the reaction, divinely conducted, has completed itself, the throb and thrill of life is an exquisite sensation. Then prayer is no more a wail, but a welcome relief to the man whose burden of death has given way to the swift-bounding step of prayerful and obedient life.

To others, there is a strong sense of being led. They were in an Egypt and knew no way to Canaan. There was a pillar of fire and cloud. They were the subjects of a divine guidance. By a conspiracy of circumstances, the way was opened. This book read, that interview enjoyed, the song that began to sing itself in the soul, the sharp sentence that had in it the portable wisdom of the ages,—by these myriad ways of environment and guidance, God has opened the gate of life to them. In his wonderful allegory, Bunyan has made a human soul start on a pilgrimage. Through various experiences it passes, but there is always guidance over a prescribed road. And running through the whole conception is the idea of the wish and the will of the King, to which there must be submission. Even when we recognize not a little of the human instrumentality, there is an overruling, so that we are divinely led. It sometimes takes even the form of being "sent," of being called of God to a work or a mission. The sphere may be lowly or large. We are set in it to do a work. Life gets to be no more accidental, because it is now providential. And the soul's inquiry, in deepest and most reverent prayer, is, "Lord, what wilt thou have me to do?" Thenceforth life has had a dignity and a purpose; and all this has been in exact moral reaction from the old unconcern. The new mission involves the idea of one who sends, and guides and gives success. Christ's words about a "Comforter" whom he would send, become precious, and prayer rises from an earnest soul for the perpetual "Presence" who is to abide with us.

But one of these more powerful personal reactions is found in those cases where the sin-consciousness compels prayer. To class one's self among sinners would have been as abhorrent as among criminals. Indeed, God had been not so much denied, as ignored as the standard of moral being. But there came to be the sense of sin. It was not the result of logical conceptions of God and duty. For the truest feelings of our human nature are often blind. They exist not as logical deduction from statements mathematically precise concerning God and immortality. But they come in upon the soul, as love comes in to man or woman in the bond that ripens into marriage. So rise some of the strongest and noblest emotions of the soul. The sense of the "I ought," than which nothing is more vital morally, is at such hours singularly strengthened. It may carry all before it. It is revealed to the soul what that sense of the "I ought" involves. And there is guilt distinctly felt, in that, whereas other principles of our nature have had due play allowed them, this kingliest consciousness of them all has had no fit hearing and following. This is not only seen but felt as sin against self and toward the God whose nearness to the soul, and whose revelation in the soul, only half recognized before, is now discerned. All this has been more than a mistake. And the sin-consciousness is borne in upon the soul. Nor are these only ignorant men who are thus exercised. Some of the noblest men in every intellectual line of work, have been so moved upon. Plain men, too, whose testimony to the fact has been a thousand times given, are on the list of those who have felt this "sense of sin." They are neither on the one hand absolutely ignorant, nor on the other liable to urge an experience into a conformity to a theory. They make our best moral witnesses, when we appeal to the consciousness of human nature on any question where such testimony is desired. And it turns out that such men, in a reaction from a former state of indifference, have felt justly concerned; have been, as they ought to be, burdened and distressed about this accumulated wrong. It has pressed prayer from lips that had not been used to pray. And when relief has come in conscious forgiveness, many have witnessed the moral phenomena and have said, "Behold, he prayeth." The result has been long years of clearer moral vision, a keener conscience has been established as the guardian of the soul from moral ills, and prayer has had its long record of gracious answer. The philosophy of this change comes, like all philosophy, after a recognition of the facts. It might be true if man were only an orderly machine, that all questions of God, Bible, duty, sin and salvation, have their logical settlement and precedence. But in fact man is more like a living organism than a machine. We love before we examine critically the emotion; we study after we feel. And in our human nature there are certain moving principles on which we act before we can get material to study the action within. And the reality of moral change, and the rising of these moral feelings of sin forgiven, of death become life, of straying feet led along a loftier path of moral living,—all these are phenomena involving prayer at every step, the answers to which are recorded on the imperishable tablet of the soul itself.

And this matter of prayer once established as a fact on one's experience, will throw a certain glow over all life. The prayerful mood is most beneficent—one might almost say munificent—for it enriches alike mind and heart. It opens, also, the vast treasure-house of God's word, and makes a man free to all its glorious surplus of spiritual wealth. The prayerful mood appropriates where the prayerless mood only speculates. It brings the treasure within one's grasp, and holds it as a personal possession. And one finds that there is no situation in life in which one cannot find, in God's Word, a promise to plead in prayer which exactly meets his need. The devout heart adores while it wonders at promises so pertinent that they seem written for one's own self—God's voice to one's own soul. And the Scripture tells us to "continue instant in prayer," to "watch unto prayer," and that "men ought always to pray." "Prayer," says Jeremy Taylor, "is the peace of our spirit, the stillness of our thoughts, the evenness of our recollection, the rest of our cares, the calm of our tempest." And what are such words but the definition of that phrase, "a devout man that prays always."

Nor, if we think of prayer as a state, rather than the act of pleading a promise, shall we have any view that is inconsistent with special seasons of peculiar prayerfulness. Sir Fowell Buxton writes, "I have always found my prayers answered, and in almost every instance I have received what I have asked for. Hence I feel permitted to offer up my prayers for everything that concerns me." But writing of that "division" in the Commons by which Emancipation was carried, he says, "If ever there was a subject which occupied our prayers it was this. Do you remember how we desired that God would give me his Holy Spirit in that emergency? I kept that passage open in the Old Testament in which it is said, 'we have no might against this great company, but our eyes are upon Thee.' I sincerely believe that *prayer* was the cause of that division."

The history of great moral achievement abounds with these instances of men who do know that God hears and answers prayer. The usual praying mood was fanned into a flame, and want lent wing to petition. "The effectual fervent prayer of a righteous man availeth much."

CHAPTER IX.

THE CIRCULAR MOTION OF PRAYER.

PRAYER, if we may use a word taken from physics, is circular in its motion. It begins in God. It comes outward and onward and downward in its curve. It passes, in the lower point of the circumference of the circle, through our souls, taking up into its sweep our personality, employing alike our wish and our want, our dependence and our freedom; and, burdened with our adoration and petition, it rises again to him who is both its Author and Finisher.

Mathematicians describe the curve as the line of beauty, and the circle as the perfection of curves. But naturalists are also claiming for the circle that all things in nature tend thereto. It is the type to which the tufted moss hidden away in lowliest dell and the grandest oak, monarch of the forest, are both trying evermore to conform themselves. Every plant, in stem, in leaf, in flower, tends, more or less, to the curve; and its whole orderly procession is also circular as it goes its round from root up through growth of fibre and comes on to seed. The year rings the trees with new wood and bark. The curved earth is swept by winds which, as they move on the line of curvature from equator to pole, have also, each storm for itself, the spiral motion. Each wave stirred by these winds rolls in a majestic curve, while the cyclones that sweep the plains are also rotary in their movements. That evolution of nature, of which our philosophical naturalists have so much to say, is not claimed to be an advance along straight lines, but the advance is by circles that overlap each other; their connection that of the links of a chain, each separate yet all attached. In the sky the planets have their vast swing in circles, and the comet, that seems a lawless intruder wandering at will, is formed to curve about the sun. In each human body there is the cycle by which we sleep and wake, adapting itself to the diurnal revolution of the earth. And as the earth never cuts exactly the same plane, but there is a slight variation that makes progress possible, so by a slight variation from year to year, we get the growth of the human body, and by-and-by, its recession and degradation in death. Mental progress comes under the same law in the individual man, and we are being moulded and rounded by influences that press in one way at the beginning, and in another in the ripeness of our intellectual life. The generations do their work of contributing to the world's progress in the same way, and all human thought grows because it swings. Yet the swing is so controlled that it endangers never the stability of our humanity, and we have it for a proverb that "history repeats itself." Civilization, starting in the East, so illustrious as the cradle and earlier home, not only of man himself but of all those arts and sciences that dignify and adorn the race, has swept onward, itself a circle, until it passes about the globe. But there has been the wheel within the wheel. For separate nations have risen and have run their round under the more vast sweep of the greater circle. Each nation in turn has touched the top, then the curve of retrocession has been observed, and then each has gone downward, often as rapidly as it rose.

Surely there is something remarkable about all this. It is more than a hint. It is a teaching. It prepares us to find that in prayer also, the Inspirer and the Hearer are One.

But the avoidance of the straight line is not more marked in mathematics and in nature than in morals. The motion of moral thought is especially instructive. An Eden, if we had it not in historical document, might be argued from the moral powers of man as man. True he is now a sinner. Broken shaft and fallen capital and the glorious remnant of the ruin, all tell of what must have been in the palmy day of pristine magnificence. His body, naturalists tell us, is one which takes in all the types furnished by lower order; but it gives prophecy of no higher being to succeed him on earth. His mind has that kind of intelligence which works by reason, than which no higher kind can be conceived of by us. His soul is capable of moral sovereignty, of holding in the right hand the sceptre of righteousness. He is a regal being in that he can, with God, rule over his sphere of being, putting all things in that sphere under the law of eternal right. Then there must have been a garden where, in the strong simplicity and vigor of oriental phrase, it may be said that "God walked with man in the cool of the day." "God created man upright." But he fell from his first estate, and there is not anywhere on earth a human soul that has not felt the result of that sin. But there was early promise, lest the race should lose heart.

Schiller has said, "The fall was a giant stride in the history of the human race." And a great orator has said that "the fall was a fall upward." Both utterances, if always it is understood that we read into them God's plan of rescue through redemption, are less startling than they first appear. The descending circle will, in the fulness of times, assume an upward curve. And the circle itself also circles about a higher purpose and we rise to an elevation greater than that from which we had fallen.

We talk of the moral progress of the human race; and rightly. Yet every gain has been by loss. And the survival of the fittest means the destruction of the unfit. So that in morals and religion we have the history of buried opinions out of which, phœnix-like, come new and better manifestations. The grand old civilizations, with kingdoms in them monarchical in form, bearing the honored name of Egyptian, Assyrian, and Babylonian, held each a truth somewhat in advance of all that preceded them. They were a grade higher than what they supplanted. But they could not live up to their own light. The retrograde motion always in sin brought each of these old nationalities down to death. The truth given them survived though they died. It is last year's leaf rotted to mould which ministers to this year's life. A nation inevitably recedes, left to itself. It climbs on the ascending curve only as it takes up God's thought. Nations always tend to run down. A force from the outside, sometimes a little higher, sometimes vastly superior, must be thrust in to conserve them. Salt has perfect saltness only in the Gospel. But the saline power is felt before Christ comes, in the thought which God sends among the nations to "prepare the way of the Lord." The rise of Greek civilization and letters is a wonder and a mystery to those who do not see it as a providence. It caught up and preserved all that it could carry and use. Plato taught at Athens because he first studied at Heliopolis on the Nile. Grateful at the theft that is never ignoble, Athens conserved and beautified as well as originated. At the height of her glory the strange and contradictory force of emigration set in, and the Greek swarmed the seaports of the Mediterranean, giving language, as Rome gave law, to the world. It is for a study to those whose curiosity is sanctified by religion, to trace out the evolution of divine purpose, and the rich fruitfulness of national preparation for the Advent of Christ. All forms of thought gave tribute as they prepared the world for His coming who was to be the Second Adam, and to bring back a better Eden than that we had lost. The cycle came round, in the fulness of times. But if the preparation was immense in one direction, the displacement was as great in another. The earlier home of the race was well-nigh deserted when the

Second Adam came. If the morning came to Western, it was because the night came to Eastern Asia. And when the Gospel, which gave the Asiatic the first opportunity, was by him rejected, its historic course was hurried on by the angel who sent the message from Europe, "come over into Macedonia and help us." And the disciples went, and the older continent relapsed into semi-barbarism; and Africa, along the shores of which, in the earlier Christian centuries, the beacon fires of Christ's religion were lighted, but whose central nations rejected the rising light, became for centuries the Dark Continent. While, on the other hand, Gaul and Britain, formerly savage wilds of savage races, received the new light and came up to lead the world along the radiant path of these latter centuries.

And here again we ask, is there not hint, suggestion, prophecy, in all this singular moral movement? Would it not be strange if all other moral things working in these ways of revolution, prayer should be the grand exception, it alone having no part in what has been called so happily "these charmed circles of moral motion?"

The peculiar experience by which men become Christians shows the same great law. They are "convinced of sin." Led to consult the Bible, they find the command, "Repent, for the kingdom of heaven is at hand." Let us suppose a man to obey this command. He is ushered into the new moral sphere which involves a new set of facts, truths, and principles. In theory, a man should have first established each point of intellectual religion, and then proceeded to make each one of them vital to the soul. But in fact, the process is often reversed, and the man comes round to logical views through the processes of the heart. He has time to justify subsequently the fact of his mingled humility and manliness. For he finds law leading back to Gospel and the Gospel leading up to law. Sin he finds as the fact on which is posited salvation. To be wrecked is the condition of being saved. To be lost is the necessity unto being found. The whole system of things has these strange correlations. Moral truths go in pairs. The new regeneration is of man and equally of God; the utmost exertion of human powers is consistent with the utmost gift of God's Holy Spirit. And never are the highest powers of man exercised apart from the operation of that divine gift. Now all this experience involves corresponding religious truth. This going backward in repentance is unto a going forward by faith; this going out of self is for the getting in under the sway of another,—all of which means that the entire moral system of things is adapted to give to a man a change of heart and change of life. For the "repentance" is a turning of one's self away and the "conversion" is a turning directly about. The system involves a Christ who goes through a similar process of retrogression and then of exaltation. We learn of him as leaving heaven for earth, then leaving earth for heaven; of his humbling of himself that he might be exalted; of his submission to all law when he was with us—law of which he himself was the Author. By suffering he redeemed us from curse. And that phrase "a suffering Saviour" in itself were a contradiction, did it not span all the wide distance between the human and the divine nature in him. It shows, as well the depths of sorrow touched for us on the one hand, and the heights of glory to which we are lifted by him, on the other. Everywhere salvation is a circle; everywhere moral motion is revolution, is rotation. God works in cycles. The fall comes round to Paradise, the garden is primal in Genesis, the City of God is the finial in Revelation. The first words of John's Gospel are the complement of the first words of Moses' history. What God the Father begins in the Old Testament, God the Son finishes in the New. Life commences in the fiat of God and completes itself in the incarnation of Jesus. If a writer on geology might happily say that the science of his love "presents itself with the magnificent spectacle of immense creations travelling in a cycle and returning to the source of their being," how much more may a student of God's Word rejoice in the immense combinations of spiritual facts and the sweep of those procedures which show God foreseeing the end from the beginning, and working all discoveries and achievements of man, and all his own special methods of grace and mercy as well, in vast circles, according to the purpose of his will which he purposed in Christ Jesus before the world began.

If then prayer be an ordained factor toward such results, like all things else, it must have its cycle. Its sweep starts out from the firm hand of God, up to which it at length returns.

In a wonderful passage of the Scripture we are taught "the Spirit helpeth our infirmities: for we know not what we should pray for as we ought; but the Spirit itself maketh intercession for us with groanings which cannot be uttered. And he that searcheth the hearts knoweth what is the mind of the Spirit, because he maketh intercession for the saints according to the will of God."

The passage is an argument. It claims that prayer has celestial beginning as well as ending; that God cannot deny himself; that what the

Spirit incites the Father must hear; that what the Spirit puts into the heart of the praying man must be known to him to whom the prayer is addressed; that prayer is more than human petition, being prompted by God; that the things asked, when we pray truly, are those which he incites us to ask in order that he may bestow them; that the soul submitting itself to the motions of the Spirit is guided in the things desired; that man's voluntariness in prayer is not lessened because there is also, equally, voluntariness on the part of God; that the mind of a devout man and the mind of the Spirit work as one in the petition, and that God cannot refuse what he inspires; and that the mind of the Spirit and the mind of God work alike in the asking and in the answer. We can argue forward or backward; forward from the prayer, or backward from the answer; and both results meet in God.

If any man shall urge that the prayer of a man should not move the Great God, here is the answer; for God moves the prayer. If any say, man is too feeble, here is the answer; for here is the might of God put first into petition and next into response. If any shall say that prayer presumes, here is the proof that the presumption would be on the part of him who should urge that God could not or would not be as much the inspirer as the hearer of man when he obeys the command, "thou, when thou prayest, enter thy closet and pray unto thy Father, and thy Father shall reward thee."

Paul's wondrous circular argument not only meets all objections, but it grandly assures one to see that God *must* "know the mind of the Spirit" in "making intercession according to the will of God." So that the line of the poet is the best commentary on the verse of the apostle:

> " Prayer is the breath of God in man
> Returning whence it came."

And this conception of prayer as circular in its movement is confirmed by many a chosen text of the Word of God. The mechanism—to use a further word drawn from physics—of prayer is clearly set forth in the Book of Daniel. We see the circle at the point of its circumference where it touches and takes up the prophet's cry as a personal force. He says "while I was yet speaking," in prayer, "Gabriel, *being caused* to fly swiftly, touched me and said, 'O Daniel, at the beginning of thy supplication the commandment came forth and I am come to show thee; for thou art a man greatly beloved." Notice that the prayer, not at its ending alone, but at its starting, has celestial impetus. The commandment came forth with the prayer; the answer begins with the beginning of the petition, and the petition is itself a part of the answer. He has only knelt, and begun to adore. The waiting angel is there before a sentence is framed. Counsel, strength, direction, and acceptance are all bestowed at outset as well as at close. His beginning and ending, his answer and petition, could almost have been reversed in their order. So elsewhere we have it, "praying in the Holy Ghost;" and in another place, the opposite statement, "The Spirit maketh intercession for us." Never the man more active than in such hours. Never is it more his own true prayer than when "led by the Spirit" to pray. It is by His grace that we are delivered from the "spirit of bondage," and made free to pray,—the old suppressed instincts of the soul, liberated from the burden that oppressed them, and the deepest feelings of our real manhood gaining freedom to voice themselves unto God.

Nor is the other side of the great fact less instructive. Are we free so that the prayer is *our* choice, our will, our plea, offered in our *utmost freedom?* None the less is God free to act upon is with an intensity that makes the prayer more than the inspiration of our own souls. The soul he is free to select for his consecrating energy, can be made by Him a "temple of the Holy Ghost." There are longings that cannot be clothed in human language. One is startled with the words which the Scriptures use about being "filled with the Spirit," "praying in the Spirit," "filled with the fulness of God."

And so the happy circle completes itself. We are bidden to "ask and knock;" but it is just as true that God knocks and asks of us that we will "open the door" that he may "come in." "Then shalt thou call and the Lord shall answer; thou shalt cry and he shall say 'here am I.'"

"Every inmost aspiration is God's angel undefiled;
And in every 'O My Father' slumbers deep a 'Here, my child!'"

CHAPTER X.

THE LORD'S PRAYER AS THE MODEL PRAYER.

THE prayer usually known as the Lord's Prayer is to be regarded rather as a generous model, than as a prescribed form from which it were a sin to deviate. It was the prayer for the hour. The disciples had asked to be taught to pray; for John had lectured to his immediate followers about true prayer. Jesus gives them the well-known words. Barely within the lines of the new dispensation, the prayer does not contain, except by implication, requests from God which Christians, farther on, were not only permitted but commanded to offer at the throne of grace. It even omits that which our Lord subsequently taught was so important, the asking "in his name." His own prayer with his disciples, just before he suffered, shows us larger ranges of prayer common to him and open to us, in which we are to imitate him; and this last prayer could with greater propriety be called "The Lord's Prayer."

As a model prayer suited to its time, it demands study, and the literature which has gathered about these few choice words is very large. It is not of that ejaculatory style of petition in which Jesus himself, and his disciples, occasionally indulged. It is a deliberate, calm, and carefully arranged petition. It suits the morning hour when the mind is at its best working, and the soul is reverent, exalted, graceful, and exultant. It is the prayer that surveys. It sees God and man, and self and sin, and grace and glory. It looks heavenward, but is not ecstatic; and earthward it looks, but is not sordid. It is simple—the child's best prayer. It is comprehensive—the range is all the way from heaven to earth, and all along the centuries of time. It is the unit of a circle in its motion, ending where it began; for its last sentence, "Thine is the kingdom," might have been given next to "Our Father in heaven" and the logical order of the thought would not have been disturbed.

It opens with devout ascription. The first sentence is the prayer *addressed*. It says it is about to ask of God; and it recognizes Him not as immanent but as enthroned; as near, or we should not ask; as far above us in the heavens, or we should not bring worship. The word "Father" conveyed to every oriental far more of the idea of sovereignty than of paternity. The prayer is not in its opening word irreverently familiar. Nor has it any new term to apply to God. The Jews, following their Scriptures, were wont to call God their Father. But the name comprehended, for those disciples, all Old Testament names; and as they should recall the fact that he had used the word "Father," rather than any narrower word such as "Almighty" or "Eternal" or "Ruler" or "Judge," and as they should see the word he actually chose, in the fuller light of the ante-pentecostal days, the word would grow on them, and the relation in which they stood to God would not be the less reverential that it is especially filial.

The prayer does not rush forward our human wants into prominence. It stops awhile with God, to revere and adore. For, that his affairs should be made a success is infinitely more important than that any of ours should be prospered. They make a mistake who think that prayer is only petition. True, there is no prayer without asking. But there is such a thing as asking God to accept our reverence. They who criticise human prayers because "they tell God so much about Himself that He knows better than we do," are forgetful of the fact that even when we address a man of high official position, we employ words that recognize his station, and we remind him of that in his situation and relations to us which makes it fitting for us to present our request. "Hallowed be thy name. Thy kingdom come. Thy will be done." These are not regarded, usually, so much as petition, as devout adoration of God in himself and his divine methods. It may be better, with many of the best scholars, to call them not petitions at all. It is reverent acknowledgment, asking leave to utter itself as best it may, and so to gain acceptance as the soul's worship of its God.

But those who hold the words "hallowed be Thy name" to be the only ascription, would see the first *petition* of the prayer in the phrase "Thy kingdom come. Thy will be done in earth as in heaven." They find similar words elsewhere which are direct petition, and ask why they are not a supplication here also. Let us not stop the flow of devotional feeling by any contention. Let any man who will, "ask" in these words; nor let him deny the right of others to find in them that thing higher than mere petition, the highest possible flight of devotion that is ever experienced on earth—a kind of prayer that meets and mingles with the angels' worship,—perhaps the first words of our first prayer when, just within the veil, our eyes "see God."

But there can be no doubt that the words "give

us this day our daily bread" are petition. Here, at least, we *ask* for something. And those who make it the earliest request in the prayer, are swift to point out its appropriateness. In Genesis, Moses does not put man's soul first, as an ancient Greek, or as a modern metaphysician, would have done, but describes man's body at the outset, because not only it was historically first, but because "our foundation is in the dust." So, here it is, in this prayer. The spiritual can wait awhile. God exalts the human body and provides its "bread." Man's body is never vile and low in the Scriptures. The unfortunate translation in the Received, is corrected in the Revised, Version; and we read, "the body of our humiliation." The Lord Jesus came in *body*, and knew bodily want. Super-spiritual men, whose only idea of religion makes it a thing of the soul, may well wonder how, on their theory, our Lord should have so stooped as to say one word about "our daily bread" in this great prayer. But God's view is wider than man's narrowness. In the era in which God made man, he made corn. It has no geological past. God charged himself with introducing the food for the newly created being. And he has cared for "seed time and harvest" ever since. Unlike the grasses, the grains are annuals. Corn never grows wild. It has no primitive type. It is abnormal, in that, in its useful state, it is not the product of cultivation. It is the most transient of the things on which we depend for food. Never is there enough of it in store to last the world for any succeeding year. God has it, as against more foes than would despoil anything else, in his own especial guardianship. The world's stated supply of it is always from hand to mouth, and has to be provided by an unslumbering providence, such as is exercised about nothing else; or the world would starve. Nothing is so precarious; yet, inside the promise, nothing more certain than the corn "for the food of man." It is, then, the fit petition, "give us this day"—or, as in the other utterance of this prayer, "day by day"—our daily bread." The mistaken spirituality of a former century made nothing of the body, and would have put the clause in the Lord's prayer about "bread" into the background. The equally false naturalism of our time, has swung the pendulum just as far the other way, and made the body the all. God's truth recognizes the body as related to the soul. The child's body must grow, and the multitudinous youthful population of the planet need food for the body as the very first thing. But does not the ripened manhood of the world need, for its own sustenance, a body duly sustained? Can the man go forth to labor, of either hand or brain, except the body be first fed? Insufficient nourishment of the body injures the mind and the soul as well. A man can think and pray better, if his body be put into good condition by good food. A new study of our Lord's discourse about "fasting" would not only correct some popular errors on that matter, but show that his teaching was not in conflict with the prayer "give us this day our daily bread." All supply of physical want is symbolized by the bread so needful for man. All bodily needs have a place in this prayer. Think of how the great populations of the world are stirring night and day to appease natural hunger! Think how the hard and horny hand of want is laid on the heads of the great toiling masses of the world! The majority of the Asiatic and African peoples do not taste meat twice a year. The race, as a race, has had no plenty aside from severe toil.

Then, too, what were food apart from appetite —appetite which may be weakened and lost by sickness? So that the prayer for "bread" covers all physical health and disease, all questions of sanitation and medicine; all the husbandmen's labor, and all the traders' industry, and all lines of commerce, whereby men earn their daily food.

Nor can we wonder that the great social questions of wage and work, of "living and of letting live," the recognition of others' rights as well as our own, are seen, by our more careful Christian economists, to get answer in the mood of mind involved when we offer this clause of the prayer. It is not "my Father" and "my bread." It is "our Father," "our bread," "our trespasses." The selection of the plural is remarkable. It cannot have been an accident. It was not in accord with most of the Biblical prayers. Not so prayed Abraham, nor David, nor Isaiah. Jesus did not so pray himself, elsewhere. There is a purpose in it. The brotherhood idea is here. The race is a unit. Its wants are one. Its sorrows are mutual. Its sins are alike. This is the prayer of men rather than of a man. Bread is sent to no one alone. "No man," in earning it, "liveth to himself." That other man, over the way, has the right to work for it, as he has to pray for it, with us. And God may send it to him so that he may share it with me, or to me so that I may share it with him. To work truly is to pray truly. "Give us this day our daily bread" is morning prayer to be offered before we go out to continue the prayer by our work. "Prayer," says the old monk, "is a trinity; for there is the prayer of the heart, the prayer of the lips, and the prayer of the life. Either member of this trinity wanting, all the divinity is gone out of the prayer."

Recall what has been urged about the corn of the earth, that it is abnormal among vegetables, needs not and cannot be developed from original wild types, as in the case of other useful plants, that it is always an annual and that it began to be at or near the time when man was ushered upon the planet, so that it is linked with him,— and, recalling all this, can we be surprised at the words " give us our daily bread "? Man's toil in preparing the earth for corn, and in sowing and harvesting it, is a sort of mute prayer. And the waving fields of the glad autumnal time are a kind of divine answer to the world's supplication. Because it needs to be newly grown each year, because there is never enough left over to feed the race, the prayer for it is to be as constant as the divine care which is needed to preserve it. And when the golden ears glow in the ruddy October sunlight, each one of them is a distinct answer from God to human prayer.

Some would have us see, in the prayer for our daily bread, a supplication also for our spiritual sustenance. But this is a mistake. We may no more crowd meaning into Christ's words than empty them of meaning. Let them stand as he set them—a prayer for the body and its food. But, then, it is not wrong to remember how always common words had in them, for our Lord, the happy suggestion. The crowd one day spoke of the bread "Moses gave from heaven;" and he spoke instantly of himself as "the Bread of Life." For the final ends must be moral ends. The earthly bread is help toward gaining the heavenly. It is a very remarkable thing that Our Lord does not tell us here to be thankful for it, when he bestows our daily bread. And the reason would seem to be that he goes back of the time when it has been given; starting in his conception with the time when it is not yet granted; starting with the moment before we can ask it; and telling us that back there, when God's hands are full but not yet opened, we may do our asking before he his giving. But, when the man has asked and God has given, then the recipient may be depended upon to be grateful. It must not be that he shall depend in vain on our gratitude.

The next clause of the wonderful prayer is connected with that about our daily bread by a copulative. "*And* forgive us our debts." Some one has happily said that all prayer can be compressed into two words, "Give" and "Forgive;" "*Give* us our bread," and "*forgive* us our debts."

That word "debts"—elsewhere given as "sins"

—has troubled not a few good men. A little thought upon its derivation would reveal its singular fitness. A debt is what is due. It is that which is owed. We owe all dutifulness to God, but we are in terrible arrears. It should have been paid. It was not, and therein is the sin. This default in duty, this delinquency, ever accumulating, becomes a debt to God which can never now be paid by us.

No amount of guilty suffering can now expiate it. For a guilty being can never render holy atoning sorrow. He can only be punished. But his punishment, though owed for the penalty, can never pay the holy obligation of the obedience due. We cannot pay the just debt to God by any suffering or future service. The sin must be forgiven. Some have wondered that there was not inserted after the word "forgive" some single phrase, such as "for Christ's sake." But this is to forget that the prayer was the prayer for that time, rather than for the time after the death of the Lord and the enlightening gift of the Holy Spirit. The word "forgive" is enough to start all thought and stir all inquiry. For the thinkers of the world, in all the great religions, have declared the impossibility of the forgiveness of a sin. Judicial minds see the immense difficulties. It seems to many persons that, outside of the Christian facts, the difficulties are absolutely insoluble. No; Christ's word "forgive" is the very word for that stage of the dawning of the New Dispensation. If a human soul cannot see as yet—as those disciples could not at that time—the infinite reason that can justify God in forgiving sin, still let the seeking soul believe that unless Jesus had seen it, and had known that the reason availed with God, he would not have had a man cry "forgive us our sins." It is enough, in certain positions, to accept the bare facts on testimony, and to drop on our knees and ask believingly for God's forgiveness.

And the added test of our asking rightly is "as we forgive," or, as some would render it, "as we have forgiven." If some see here the measure, others see, with better vision, the indispensable condition, not indeed so much with God, as with ourselves. Our forgiveness of others is not the infinite reason why God forgives us; but it is the proof that we rightly ask. If we ask, when living in the consciousness of any cherished sin, whether in feeling or act, against others, we are withholding a due, a debt, a wage, a work, a right, from others. In that case we ask amiss. And God, answering our prayer, would be partaker of our sin. And therefore it is that the phrase about "our bread" is joined by the copulative "and" to the phrase "forgive us our debts." And there is added thereto the phrase "for we forgive;" thus making out of the three phrases one sentence. So that it is everywhere a test of true asking that we shall never ask in the interests of wrong. Never, holding an unkind mood of mind to a brother man, can we ask God to be kind to us. Nor must we wait for an enemy to make reparation and atonement. For, what an Infinite God, acting in this capacity of righteous Governor of the universe, may demand in the case of a subject, is one thing; and the duty of two men to each other, as brother men on the same plane of equality of being, both often sinners, is another thing. We are to forgive a fallible brother, as ourselves tempted, and as those in some other matter in need of forgiveness from our fellow-man.

Note the careful order in which the petitions to "give" and to "forgive" are followed by the petition to "lead." "Lead us not into temptation." It is the cry of weakness and fear lest we should, even when forgiven, be left to ourselves. If, at first glance, we are surprised that the petition does not take the positive form, and ask to be "led by the Spirit," we have only to remember again, the time when this prayer was put into the lips of the twelve. Pentecost had not yet shown its tongues of flame. The near thing was trial, and testing, which was by means of evil. The prayer is not for exemption from any contact with temptation. It does not ask that we may be delivered from the temptation, but from the actual evil of yielding to it. The testing is in a fallen world. The prayer recognizes the trend of a weak though forgiven soul. It is a prayer that we may be kept. It has been happily paraphrased in this way: "Suffer us not to be led into the temptation by which we shall fail, but lift us up out of the dominion of evil." Then comes the rounding up of the petition, which indeed some would omit. But the omission makes the ending abrupt, while the ordinary version brings us again to the lofty mood where the prayer began.

And so the prayer, singularly simple for infant lips, yet profound enough to be beyond all our measure, continues to be repeated the world round and the ages through. Now, in our want, we emphasize the one part, and, anon, the other. At one time we revel in its devout ascriptions, at another rejoice in the requests it permits us to offer, at still another time we are almost overwhelmed in its wonderful comprehensiveness. There it stands, recognized by lisping childhood, strong manhood, and ripened age. Its grand calmness, so unlike the fervent repetitions of the Hebrew prayers of its age, and its practical petitions that God would "give," "forgive," and "lead," its breadth covering all the distance from the Father on the throne to man in his weakness and want, spanning too the centuries from the beginning of "the kingdom" until its fulness shall "come," all these make it the model prayer of the Christian dispensation.

CHAPTER XI.

SUPPOSED LIMITATIONS OF PRAYER.

There are some things about prayer which are thought to be its limitations, but which are really its extensions.

These limitations are supposed to come either from our human frailty on the one side, or from the divine perfection on the other. It may be said that, since man is always faulty, so he must be often in error in his prayers. And, also, it is said that, since God's will is perfect, and since we are to add to every prayer the codicil, "Thy will be done," we do in so far limit our prayers as to ask little or nothing that we really wish or want; so that it were about as well not to ask at all, but only to take what is sent.

Now, it is true that the praying man is faulty, and that he may "ask amiss." The perfect theory of prayer is that it is a voluntary human petition, to which one is moved by the Holy Spirit sent forth from the God who intends to answer the requests he has inspired. But the human factor introduces an element of imperfection. And this fact must modify the working of the theory. Hugh Miller complains of those "whose unscientific gunnery never takes into account the parabolic curve of man's fallen nature." Our human wish mingles with God's Holy Spirit in shaping our prayer. And man may not always be able to separate the two. A praying man may find the unexpected answer to his petition in the sudden flash that comes to him on his knees, and shows him that his motives were too human. Infirmity has played too large a part in his petition. He may see with dismay his former motives as singularly mixed and unworthy. There has been more of self than of the Spirit. And this man shall pray now with cleaner heart. And the outcome shall be a purer supplication, and one more completely under the leadings of the divine Inspirer. The things desired, he was permitted to mention. And the result has been a lesson in self-knowledge. The specific thing has been denied. A child begged permission to handle the serpent. Its beauty had fascinated him as he saw it glide so easily by, with its folds of green and brown, its keen eye glittering like a jewel. He begged. He prayed. He entreated. He became frantic. He charged his father with unkindness in not allowing him to seize the serpent. All the time the father refused. But when, in after-years, the story was told to the boy now grown to manhood, he thanked his father for the denial. God keeps away from men the shining good they had so ardently desired. It seemed to them a real blessing. They prayed for it. The prayer seemed legitimate. The motive was not consciously unworthy. There was no mixture of evil present to the mind. But the earnestness of the petition was seen afterward to be mainly human fervor. And the answer was a restriction, in one way, but an enlargement in another. For the pitying God gave the suppliant wider vision; and he was taught a lesson that could be learned in no other way. The nameless mother of Zebedee's children, modest for self, was ambitious in her request for her sons. She may have thought herself actuated by the best of motives. Her parental love mingled with her faith. She believed in "the kingdom." A praying mother, she thought her boys would help the Lord's cause in their natural nobility. She had trusted them. She thought the Master needed about him trustworthy men. But Christ's words, gently uttered, showed her herself. The answer was less restricted than the prayer.

So, too, there is a range of things about which there is no special promise. Men are not made infallible by the Holy Spirit. They are to ask to be guided. They may pray over the question of a trade to be learned, or an investment to be made. Not to pray in these cases would be a sin. They may ask God to indicate the profession to be studied, the business to be undertaken; to indicate the city or township in which to locate. They may inquire of him whether their life-work is to be done on one continent or on another. There are surgeons who never make an incision in a dangerous case, without a lifted prayer for divine aid and blessing. There are men who would no more think of going into a new business without prayer than without capital. Sometimes, to be allowed to make a mistake may be the best possible answer to request for guidance. A man may learn more by a failure than by an immediate success. And as the ultimate ends of life are moral, it may be that a man, however shrewd and however prayerful, shall be ordained to God to fail in the temporal that he may gain in the spiritual life. Or there may be a mistake made in interpreting providential indications. There is no infallibility. But this is not to say that there is no guiding response. A man may have learned the wrong lesson. The response may have been missed because answer comes from an unexpected quarter of the sky. The leading may not tally with the wish. For it is by no means the case of a blind man whose hand is grasped by another and he led onward not knowing himself a step of the way. God's leadings have in them, often, the recognition of the intelligence with which he has endowed a man. God may be educating the man's judgment. God may be making an appeal to him to employ his own faculties, to estimate facts, and use his own will in deciding the question of what is to be done. The man wanted an overmastering impression, but God gave him, instead, a clearer intellect and surer judgment. God was compelling an intelligent decision. In place of the expected narrowness, there is breadth. Instead of restriction there is liberty and extension. A man's natural limitations and infirmities are used as an education for him. It is not only that better things are given than were asked, but that more is made of the asker. Larger moral manhood waits upon what seemed infirmity and restriction. The man who asked for blessings on himself finds blessings in himself. But there is another alleged limitation. It is said that the whole idea of prayer is that of interference and restriction. It is narrowness imposing its wish on the perfect largeness of God. It is claimed that the conception of God as independent of prayer is the broader conception of the two: that it were better that he should have his own perfect and immutable plan. And thus under the plea of honoring God the more, one would pray the less; and prayer, less in volume, would be broad exactly as it became more a recognition than a petition; more an acknowledgment of God's perfect arrangement rather than a request for him to introduce a change, which cannot be other than a restriction on his power as well as on his wisdom.

The objection runs on this wise: "God has arranged not only all events but all potencies. God has foreseen and provided for all things; and we cannot, if we would, change unalterable fact by our feeble cries." But is not the legitimate inference from these admitted premises very different from this? Nay, more; is not the fair and honest conclusion to be drawn from the fixedness of things, exactly the opposite of all this? "God has arranged all events." Yes. And arranged, if that be so, for *this*, as one of these events—that prayer shall be answered. To say the opposite is to allege that this is the event not included in the "all events" which "God has arranged." "God has foreseen all." Yes. And this is also foreseen. "We cannot change an immutable fact." True; and this fact of answered prayer is one of the immutable facts. A prayer offered is as immutable a fact as is the existence of God. The reason for the prayer is the fixed and unalterable arrangement for the hearing of it. And so the reason for praying is precisely the reason for doing anything else in a universe governed by an Omniscient and Omnipotent God. The objector on the ground that freedom is destroyed by God's planning, contradicts himself in every voluntary act of his mortal life. He confutes his own objection every time he lifts his hand in God's air or plants his foot on God's earth. If it be absurd to hope to gain anything in prayer on the ground of perfect divine purpose in all things, then it is exactly as absurd to hope to gain anything in any other sphere by aught that we can do. The objection, if valid at all on this principle, paralyzes all action in any line of human activity. If for this reason valid, it means that you should do nothing, for God does all; plan nothing, for God plans all; cease all diligence, for you can do nothing against the divine plan of things. It cuts the sinews of enterprise outside as well as inside the closet of prayer. It makes man a puppet by denying him the freedom accorded him in the plan of his God. Now, it is plain that there must be some flaw in such an inference, yet the premises are certainly right. God must be a Sovereign; and any subtraction from his sovereignty over the human will is a mistake. The human will, exercising itself in prayer, has its abundant freedom in that it is in abundant accord with God's will; and so it is in perfect voluntariness under that will, it is as free to ask as is his will to answer. The strictly logical conclusion is this, that by divine plan there is place for the prayer of man, exactly as for any other form of human exertion. In the natural world, the divine plan of things, in connection with our freedom, is the basis of all human activity. We can depend on the sun to rise and set, on the procession of the seasons, on the ordination of seed-time and harvest, and therefore we labor. We see that laws are fixed, and therefore we labor; and therefore we pray, as well. No law, there would be no prayer. Little law recognized, little prayer. Law recognized everywhere, not only in its general aspects, but in special events which are every moment transpiring about us, and the man will pray the more. The nearer God in natural law, as the sustainer and upholder of all things, the more constantly the breath of prayer will form on the lips. It was a Christian poet who sang—

> "Teach us that not a leaf can grow
> Till life from Thee within it flow;
> That not a blade of grass can be,
> O Fount of being, but by Thee."

The more laws, the more proof of God; the

more laws recognized in their general sweep and in the minuteness of the providences which transpire under them, the more prayer. The nearer and the more active God, the more we act and the more we pray. It was he who saw not a sparrow fall without the Father's notice, who spent whole nights in prayer. It is God recognized in minutest events that enables a man to "pray always." The truth would seem to be that the man who objects to prayer because of "God's immutable plan" does not at all conceive the idea of God in his own mind. He says "God," but means "nature," or "law," or "mystic force," or "unknowable power." He is not a man who sees God's plan in daily providences, in the numbered hair and the falling sparrow. If he really believed in a God who was right there, in his room, where he was writing the words "God has arranged all and therefore man need not pray," he would stop midway in his sentence, the pen would drop, and he would fall upon his knees in instant prayer. God so near, so real to him as that—and yet if God is, he is there and is so near as that—his soul within him would pray despite himself. How quickly he would speak to an eminent stranger the instant his presence was perceived in the room where he was writing. He could not but pray if God were felt to be near enough to plan and to execute his plan in the very chamber of one's most secret thought and study. Prayer is sometimes extorted from unwilling lips,—the prayer of recognition when not of affection, the prayer of compulsion, as from one's deepest conviction of its rightfulness, even when it is not the "Abba Father" of adopted sonship. A practical working faith in God's plan as to all minutest things is a marvellous incentive to prayer. And it is the undevout and not the devout soul that says "God is Omniscient, therefore I need not pray." The devout man says "God is Omniscient; therefore I pray with confidence to Him whose eye nothing can escape, and who can see what is the best answer and when the best time to grant it, and what the best measure of the gift I ask him to bestow." And we may put it without hesitation to any jury of fair-thinking men as to which man of the two is most philosophical as before the fact of an Omniscient God. For it is certain that the man who best and most thoroughly believes in an Omniscient God will best and most frequently do the philosophical act of praying. And while humblest souls may act from a holy instinct in supplicating the divine blessing, yet, on the other hand, there can be no more reasonable nor more thoughtful, nor loftier exercise of the human soul, and none in which a calm and philsophical mood is more befitting and helpful, than in the solemn, tender act of prayer to God. There will be always an unexplored remainder of mystery about prayer. Indeed, in all high exercise of the human soul there is mystery, and the mystery increases when it is the case of one soul moving another soul, and the mystery culminates when one of these persons is God. But it becomes one of that kind of mysteries which is helpful to the duty in the case of prayer. Every truth which has a Godward side runs back into a mystery that helps best the corresponding duty on the manward side. What more deep and impenetrable than the plans of God in relation to prayer? But what more simple on the human side than prayer as the cry of a child longing for the light? Let no man ask for full explanation of this or any other truth on its Godward side. Adoration of a wisdom that is necessarily hidden from us by its very breadth is our part. Confidence in him that he is right and wise when working out of our sight, is a virtue impossible to us did we completely understand him. Trusting in the dark is nobler than trusting in the light. The unseen is by no means the useless in nature or in religion. Who ever saw gravity, or electricity, or heat? In religion there is always a light from the unseen and the unknown on the things about us. The cloud appearing in the sky was dull an hour ago. But see. From away and out of your sight, down beyond the western horizon where the sun is still shining, there comes up into that dull cloud a great glory and beauty of color. It flashes across to those other clouds in the east. It gives them its own warmth and glow. The earth, on its rivers and lakes and oceans, catches the reflection from that cloud, which, after all, is only a something seen shot through by a something else that is unseen. So duty has its radiance from an unseen God, and human action, alike in prayer and work, is a better thing shot through with the divine glow of beauty and power. Man works better and prays better for God; feels larger and stronger and safer when the everlasting arms are about him, and is never so free as when God's blessed purpose enfolds and protects his freedom, nor so prayerful as when the glad mystery rises up over him and envelopes him, and he cries with the wisest soul of the olden time, "And will God indeed dwell with men!" A thing is not the less philosophical because there is mystery exactly where mystery ought to be. The unphilosophical would be to expect it nowhere, and deny that to be truth which has place for mystery. Mystery is breadth rather than limitation in any truth which runs up toward God, as does this truth of prayer.

It should be noted that the Biblical writers never feel the pressure of these alleged limitations. They are Orientals. As such they also incline to fatalism. The Oriental loves to think that all events are fixed. "Fate rules." "What is to be, will be" is the Oriental creed. But the idea of God once introduced, there is an instant change. The Scripture writers do not simply use the word "God" where other Orientals used the word "Fate." That were as small gain as to have men in our day use the word "God" instead of the word "law." But the whole conception of God in the Scriptures is that of the Ever-living God. He is the God alive to human want and awake to human petition. The deadness of Pantheism disappears before the life of God, who sits not in solitary distance, but is closely concerned in human affairs. The Oriental, believing in God, is naturally and necessarily a praying man. And the Scripture writers do not so much as name a difficulty or objection to prayer. That there is a God seems to them the sufficient reason for offering to him prayer. Prayer is the natural thing because he is the All-Wise God. To any other being, whose plan was not perfect, they could not ascribe praise or offer petition. Nor were those praying men of the Biblical times mere novices in thought. Not an objection to prayer but it must have been duly weighed and set down at its full worth by such a man as Moses—the most judicial mind of past centuries. Such a man went through all these difficulties, and did not sink like a weaker swimmer, but came out safely and stands firm on the believing side. No difficulty can be really new, except in mere form of statement. These men prayed because they thought the matter through. Praying men are more sensitive to the difficulties of prayer than any other class of men. Those great souls of the grand centuries were not mere speculators upon the theme; they followed the light, and the farthing candle became a glowing sun. The limitations disappeared. The very hindrances, duly considered, became helps. For those souls, as for us, neither the weakness of man, nor the perfectness of God, is an obstacle. Both of these facts are rather the open doors swung wide by angel hands for liberating some imprisoned Peter. To those men the one fact stood forth that God, just because he is God, is "the rewarder of them that diligently seek Him." So that the breadth which belongs always and necessarily to the idea of God, disperses completely those mists of limitation that abide with the men who do not grasp it. Prayer as a conception does not narrow the idea of God. It enlarges our conception of him. It makes alike the mystery and the knowledge of God contribute to its reverent and intelligent exercise.

All the alleged limitations to prayer, when closely scanned, become its enlargements. The mistakes and misconceptions gone, prayer is as reasonable as it is righteous, is demanded by the head no less than by the heart, is justified in its theory and commended in its practice. The more it is understood and employed, the wider appears to be its range, the swifter its wing, the surer its basis in eternal purpose, the more imperative its duty, the greater its worth to man, and the more delightful its privilege. The very study of prayer as a problem broadens one's horizon as its practice enlarges one's soul.

CHAPTER XII.

PRAYER IN ITS PROPHECY.

"ANSWERED prayers," says Dr. Theodore L. Cuyler, "cover the field of providential history as flowers cover Western prairies."

Another shall tell the story of Livingstone's death in the act of prayer that Africa might have life. "They laid him on a rough bed in the poor hut his faithful black followers had builded for him, where he spent the night. Next day he lay undisturbed. He asked a few wandering questions about the country. His faithful black followers knew that the end could not be far off. Nothing occurred to attract notice during the earlier part of the night; but at four in the morning, the black boy who lay at his door called in alarm. By the candle still burning, they saw him, not in bed, but kneeling at his bedside with his head buried in his hands upon his pillow. He had passed away on the farthest of all journeys, and without a single attendant. But he had died in the act of prayer—prayer offered in that reverential attitude about which he was always so particular, commending his own spirit, with all his dear ones as was his wont, into the hands of his Saviour; and commending Africa with all her woes and sins and wrongs to the Avenger of the oppressed and the Redeemer of the lost. And so, though Livingstone died, he was Africa's victor."*

Among the "Resolves" of Jonathan Edwards was this: "Very much to exercise myself in prayer all my life long." Arnold of Rugby told his pupils that he should offer a prayer daily before the first lesson. "Holy Samuel Rutherford," as he was called, had his out-of-doors place for prayer and said, "I prevailed; as woods, trees, meadows, and hills are my witnesses." Prayer has been the strong tap-root from which have sprung the broadening branches of moral activity in the individual soul, as well as large fruitage for Christ's kingdom among men. That prayer has a natural fertility in a special kind of results is not only a reasonable belief but an obvious fact. That "things follow their tendencies" is a clearly defined moral principle. That they have actually done so is the declaration of all history. And therefore that they will continue to do so, is a prophecy not without its significance in the matter of prayer.

---

* "Along the Pilgrimage," by Dr. Wayland Hoyt.

We have thus far studied the matter of prayer with reference to its divine answers. It remains, now, to look at the natural result of the praying mood in men. It *moulds them.* The moulding process is toward better ages for mankind, and toward preparation for heaven in the praying man.

There is obviously a kind of charm about prayer, or men would never so uniformly, through all the centuries, have done so much praying. As the prayers of the race get to be better, and purer, and more voluminous, they tend to mould human nature. Prayer cannot be stopped by any force whatsoever; but it can be ennobled, directed, and purified, and so become more forceful and beneficent in its natural effects on praying men. For prayer is both old and new. It is as old as Eden, as new as our last uplifting, in this present moment, of our own petition. It combines all the charm of antiquity with all the interest of novelty. Youth prays for wisdom, middle life for help, and age prays for heaven. Penitence prays, and faith prays, and hope prays, and joy prays. Success prays with thankfulness, disaster prays tremblingly; defeat prays, as its last resort, for one more trial this side of despair. Prayer is a crucible into which we cast those truths that are harsh and unwelcome in the creed, and find them capable of happy fusion; and many a man who disputes a doctrinal point on his feet yields his assent on his knees before God. Prayer is a brook by the way, and a staff for the pilgrim weary on the march. Prayer is a lofty promontory pressing itself out into the ocean, its top unwetted by the spray of any storm that ever blew, and hurling back any wave the ocean can raise against it. Prayer is the seaman's best bower anchor, when his vessel rides over against the toothed rocks of a frowning shore—an anchor that never gives way, "that entereth within the veil." Prayer is a great rock in a weary land; and in under the cool shadow of its overhanging roof, where tiny streams issue from the sides green with the lichens, the hot and thirsty traveller finds shelter from the heat and pure water to moisten his noontide repast. "The Lord is my Shepherd. He leadeth me beside the still waters." Prayer has its devotional sweetness, its sacred calm, its great sense of God, its open-eyed vision, its profound stir of all the soul within us. It has, at times, its agony of desire, its pleading earnestness, its very argument with God. It grows jubilant in hope and it revels with a kind of sacred abandon in the promises. At times, it turns its glass toward the skies, and has a telescopic outlook and uplook. And yet again the nearer duties of daily Christian living are made radiant by the parallel light that flashes along the surface of the field where we do our work. Prayer is now lofty and anon lowly. It sometimes gets it victories by submission, as did Jacob at the brook and Jesus in the garden. At other times it bursts into doxologies of praise, as does Paul in the midst of mighty argument, where heart escaped from brain, and would not wait for the decorous close of careful discourse. But whatever prayer may be at times, this is its chief thing, that it is a mood of mind, a spirit that takes on these various methods and manners. "I will pour out the spirit of supplication," *i.e.*, the spirit or mood of prayer, the devotional spirit.

Few gifts, perhaps none, can be named which can compare with this devotional mood of mind. It makes an atmosphere; and all the truths of religion are made transparent by the clarity of this medium. It is the light in which we see light.

The influence of the affections upon the intellect is a well-known fact. You shall find, in social life, persons not really lovely in a single feature, but who are esteemed beautiful by those who see them with fond eyes; and others, looking upon those whom we call beautiful through a prejudiced vision, declare them plain and graceless. But in moral judgments, the personal element of our own sympathy or dislike has even wider scope. Jesus spoke of men "who loved"—a word of the heart—"who loved darkness rather than light because their deeds were evil." The inner nature and the prevalent mood and tone of the soul were so out of sympathy with our Lord that the honest opinions of such were mistakes. They would not be convinced, even by the direct teachings of Jesus Christ. But when such men, under the deeper stir of their natures, have felt the desperateness of their need, and have been willing to pray, their difficulties have departed, and almost before they knew it they have accepted what they had denied. The secret is that they have come, by the processes of the heart, into Christ's kingdom. The trouble had been that they not only had looked out through colored glass, but with a diseased eye. The mist from the low-down heart has risen up into the head. The deeper nature made right, the brain works accurately and fairly. The eye restored to normal vision and the man standing out in God's pure sunlight, that brightness rather than the old darkness is now loved. In such a case the elemental steps are taken toward securing a devotional spirit.

But the process must not be arrested. There are instances where the truth intellectually received is of little moral worth because of lack of continuous prayerfulness. True religion, in part, is a study, a science, a system. But devotion is more than study. Study piles up the materials, assorts them carefully, and assigns them to their place; here these bricks are to go, and there those boards; in this part of the structure the stone and the iron. But a heap of brick and lumber is not a house, a mere pile of material is not a dwelling for man. Brawny labor may collect these different things, but taste and skill and careful work must build the structure. The mere scholar in religion may do good service in the material he brings. But if not careful, the very criticalness of his mental habit may harm his own spiritual life. For piety, as well as learning, is needed in the application of truth to one's own soul, unto the best interpretation. Heart as well as head is required. The devotional mood is essential as well as the critical method. Not alone for plain people, but for scholarly men, it is written that he that enters the kingdom must come as a little child. The arrogance of scientific opinion, the pride of learning, the impatience of any dictation, the result of the great executiveness needed and fostered in commercial success—all must go down in humble obeisance before Christ's words. Receptiveness as toward Christ's offers to be Teacher and Saviour, the attitude of the kneeling suppliant rather than that in which one stands on proudest tiptoe, is the demand. We may not patronize Christ's truth if it commends itself. We may not add to our stature in trying to reach higher than others; posing as orginal discoverers in religion, we are tallest on our knees. There are truths meant more to impress us than to instruct us. Like God's thunder, their use is to awe the soul. Ingenuity digs about them, but soon gives over the task; for it can do nothing with them. They can only be taken as God meant them to be, with a devotional spirit, that will trust where it cannot understand; that believes in them because God understands them and tells us the "what," but not the "why." All real truth in religion runs off into the infinite and so is beyond our ken. It is only the false that can be comprehended. When a party were struggling on toward the ocean, each man desirous to be the first to discover it, a straggler from an eminence cried out to those below, "I see it." The leader of the party veiled his doubt in a question, "How wide is it?" "About ten miles," was the reply. "Nay: that is not the true ocean: for no man can see across the ocean." No finite mind can see all about an infinite truth. And yet, every day, we have in religion to act in view of truth that reaches up to God and on into eternity. Salvation is through attachment of our interests to God's infinite plans of grace and mercy. Christ obtained "eternal redemption" for us. We accept the fact. The elevation of the devotional spirit is such that it can take, on trust, from God, the truths that the logical intellect can neither discover nor understand. The devotional spirit is thus our broadest mood; and so is our best preservation from that mere intellectual narrowness which would abridge the wideness of God's revelation to what our reason or intuition can determine. In such a scheme of things as those which environ a man in a gospel land, the devotional spirit is one of the best preservatives from religious error.

And this prayerful spirit is, moreover, a central citadel against the assaults of temptation. The most of our temptations come up through the gateways of passion and desire. The assault is not so much upon our principles as upon our feelings. This kind of warfare aims to do as gunners do in war, when they send their hot shot into a beleaguered city, hoping to fire the buildings or to explode the magazines, and thus induce surrender without assaulting the outer defences. Mere conscience and will are not enough. The heart must be guarded in its emotions. Men fall suddenly who had stood high for years under the protection of sentinels who guarded every outpost. But it was a sudden bombshell thrown over the guards on the walls, and coming in upon the affections, that made such havoc. Not those men who have most principle or most knowledge are the most secure, but those who possess in their hearts the most of the spirit of devotion. No amount of resolving will help a man, apart from the mood of mind that walks lovingly and truly with God in constant prayerfulness. We must guard the central magazine where is stored the powder which a spark may explode. Luther says, "The devil plagues and torments us in the place where we are the most tender and weak. In Paradise he fell not upon Adam, but upon Eve." It is not sinful to be tempted. The sin is in the yielding. God's method of dealing is to allow us to be tempted, and then to sanctify us by giving us the strength to overcome it. The temptation may be stronger than our unaided will can meet. We are not matched against infernal wiles used by one who has had six thousand years of all too skilful practice. The ordinary temptations of any man are strong enough to ruin him: each one of them has overthrown millions as good and as firm as he. And the better a man the more his temptations. Christ was tempted with kingdoms. None so suffer as those at whom Satan, because they stand so high, strikes his strongest blows. What need of tempting a wicked man? He tempts himself. Satan is fairly sure of him. It were needless to spend time and art, and spread net and snare, and solicit and seduce such an one. But if Satan can get a really good man to fall, he is filled with his infernal joy. We will set our watch on the walls. We will guard every outpost. We will strengthen our resolves. We will bring in all holy fear. We will busy our hands with willing work. We will do our utmost at resistance. But the best thing to do is to pray and pray, until we get anointed from God with the "spirit of prayer;" until the whole mood of soul is devotional, until the whole tone and temper of mind is that of a life "hidden with Christ in God."

Closely allied with the form of temptation just considered is that which comes from an unoccupied heart. The intellect may be full of truth, but the heart be desolate. Yet something must be loved. The tendrils must not grovel on the soil where the earthworm feeds upon them. The loves of the heart must be lifted into God's sun and air. The tender spiritual mood is needed; the loving nature must be maintained, the affectionate spirit be cherished. Forbidden things, painted in novel colors, will get the attention of a wandering and unoccupied eye. Golden temptations by their glitter will attract the soul unfilled with divine good. We cannot be emptyhearted. The baited hook is for the hungry mouth. How plainly a devotional spirit is one of the best shields against temptation. The defence, in this case will be just at the point of the attack. Feeling will be met by feeling; the lower by the higher, the evil spirit by the good spirit. The heart full of these contemplations of God's grace gained through a prayerful study of God's Word, will be preoccupied. Other pleasures will bar out the painted deceits of sin. Let once the devotional habit be established, and there will be a fear lest anything whatsoever should disturb the delicious joy. For habits are like ruts in the highway, and the heart goes easiest in them. And these devotional habits, this constant life of communion with God, brings us into contact with a whole world of spiritual facts that are never exhausted. They are too wide in themselves, too largely related to human life here and the eternal life beyond, ever to grow stale and flat and unprofitable. We never do much more than just to dip beneath the surface of this ocean. We never work this mine so much and so long as to exhaust all its ore. The mere intellectual conception of truth may weary, but the moral side, discoverable to the man of prayerful spirit, rests and refreshes.

It needs no argument to show that a human soul introduced, in this way, to the mind and heart of God, cannot lack for subjects of interest and impressiveness. Admitted to daily communion with "the God of all grace," it must become graciously inclined. Seeing into the bosom of God's love in its gospel manifestation, it must grow loving. This divine preoccupation must be the armor within. It must be the central life which repels all which is antagonistic. It has something to give out of its fulness, and little to take from the scanty and fallacious joys that come as tempters. The room is taken. The heart has found its natural home in God's love and grace. The prodigal soul, come back to the Father's house, has had enough of wandering. We do not read that the restored son ever returned to the husks in the far-off land. There was enough, now, all about him, in the father's home, to charm him into staying there for a lifetime.

And the mood of true prayerfulness does not nourish the solitary to the harm of the social graces. One may begin by praying to "my Father;" but he soon comes to say "Our Father." All love that has God's love in it is holy. The life-blood of piety is the devotional spirit, and it comes to be tender and true toward man as beloved of God. Much is said about the culture of human affection, of brotherhood love. But as there would be no brother save for a father, so there is no brotherhood love which is holy that does not stand in first loving the Father. Mere unsanctified affectionateness, the animal feeling for kind and kindred, we share with the brutes; and there is no religion about it. Only as the natural instinct is shot through with holy love does it rise into a religious virtue. There is no holiness in the love of a lioness for her young. It is simply natural, instinctive, and non-moral. Another element than the natural must be thrust in to lift our human affection to the rank of sanctified affection. God's love in us not only enlarges love, but purifies its source. There are diseases which seize on some special member of the body. They affect the ear or the eye. The pain is manifested now here and now there. All local remedies are vain. At length the physician begins to look back among the vital organs for the cause. No more is he successful there in his treatment. Presently he discovers that there is a defect in the blood, the central fluid of life, and begins to comprehend the fact that only as that is purified, can he reach the disease which showed itself in local troubles. All attention is now directed to this one central act; and if he can succeed in pouring through the veins of the body a fuller and richer tide of vital blood, he has made his cure. There are evils that rectify themselves when the heart is right. And though the application to a local trouble may still be needed in some cases, the new nature is there, to which we can appeal, when we would make the outer conduct correspond with the inner life. The faults of a quick temper, a peevish mood, a petulant reply, are by none more clearly seen and earnestly deplored than by those who are striving, notwithstanding these infirmities, to subdue all things to the dominion of Christ. Never does a man see these imperfections so clearly as when they are remembered on his knees. Never does he struggle against them so earnestly as when he finds that they hinder his prayer. Never does he gain such victories over them as when the peculiar devotional mood has sway, and he lives daily in communion with God. This prayerful spirit takes out the hardness and harshness and censoriousness native to some men. It warms up the natural coldness and calculation and mathematical regularity of some men's virtues. It puts a man in the way of knowing the luxury of what has been called the "abandon of goodness;" the surrender of one's self to the sacred impulses of religion. An affectionate Christian, who is neither afraid nor ashamed to allow himself the delight of sanctified feeling, is a higher style of man than he who is statuesque in his piety.

Among the habits of mind conducive to devotion is that of connecting all things with God. It sees that the little things as well as the large are under his eye. Our Lord told us that the falling sparrow and the numbered hair are held in mind by his Father. Never mind scoffers who call this childish. Never mind the extra-critical men who cry law here and law there. No matter now for your philosophical theory, whether you hold matter to have been originally endowed with potencies, or so made as to be acted upon, each instant, by direct forces which can be exercised only by mind. Let us not get befogged amid the question of first and of second causes. God is conceived of by the pious men of the Scripture as the present energy of the world. And human hearts, attuned to the divine harmonies of love, feel him near and own him the Sustainer as well as the Creator of the Universe.

When Peter and John were forbidden to speak in the name of Jesus, the early Christians "lifted up their voices to God with one accord and said, 'Lord, thou art God, which hast made heaven and earth and the sea and all that in them is.'" At first glance, such a petition seems like the stately words of a grand invocation at a great public service. But closely read, it is just the opposite. These men were going to brave the wrath of their rulers by disobedience to their order. But there was a God, who was Sovereign of the visible universe. Their appeal was away from a human to a divine Ruler. Their hope of successfully doing what was their duty, was in the Almighty God who had made "the heaven and earth and sea and all that in them is." It was the simplicity of their devotional mood that gave them such exaltation. Such a powerful, superaboundingly powerful, God was on their side. No idea had they, but that such a God, who so intimately controlled all things, would answer. The praying mood, in their case, connected all things with God. It even took in the will of their haughty rulers, since it made their arrogance the reason for God's supreme action. Those rulers were thought to be wise; but God was all-wise. Those rulers declared *their* will; God would show what *his* hand and counsel had determined before to be done. It was will against will, plan against plan; and the one who had bidden them speak had known the will of those who forbade them. Their God and Christ was intimately concerned in all things. These disciples were in no accidental position. Not a word do they say about "law"—or, if that name be new,—not a word about "the principles" of which all the thought and speech of their time was so full. It is all, God. They were embosomed with him. He is authority and appeal. His will, not their own, nor that of Jewish rulers, should be done by them. "Grant unto thy servants that with all boldness they may speak thy word." And so these men were philosophical without knowing it. For the unphilosophic mood is that which restrains prayer. To refer our life in all its events to God's arrangements, is to find material in hourly providence for the devotional spirit.

And thus is begotten a kind of moral intrepidity which is a very illustrious Christian virtue. Prayer is pledged duty. There is often seen, when in the very act of prayer, some duty which once done, is God's answer through our own act. We are given of God to answer some of our own prayers. We are bound to do our utmost for gaining the ends for which we are praying. Some things go naturally with petition. They are the "Amen" in act, of the words of prayer. There are things that comport well with the earnestness with which we plead for divine blessing. We must work for what we pray for, or we shall soon cease to pray for it. And how it stirs us to heroic effort, when in close communion with God, we seem to get in among the gracious activities of the divine mind. God is the ceaseless worker, with amazing obstacles to confront Him. God is a man of war. John saw war in heaven, and victory over mighty foes won by him whose title was "King of Kings, and Lord of Lords." Enthronement in a universe, in which for reasons known only to God, evil is permitted to organize and do its worst, is not a place of ease. The intense personal activity of God is the constant idea of the Bible. He is a foe and he has foes. It is no easy work to counteract evil in free intelligences. It required the wisdom of God to lay the plan, the power of God to execute it, the love of God in the self-denial of the Calvary cross to accomplish it, the gift of the Holy Spirit to each human soul to secure it. In some far-off eternity, when weakness, confined to the great prison-house of the universe, shall cease to rage because utterly hopeless, when not a finger shall be lifted because the final judgment day is come and gone, the placidness of God may be the theme of heavenly song. Isaac Taylor in his "Last Conflict of Great Principles," one of the finest prose poems in the language, sketches the final battle of these present antagonisms, and glances on to the time when God shall "enter into his rest." But, until then, he has "girded his sword upon his thigh." Until then he is in the midst of the battle. And for a man to be admitted, through much of prayer and study of the Word, into "the Secret of the Lord," is to hear the clash of the resounding arms, and to ask a place in the fight "on the Lord's side." It is for a man to be strong in the faith of the final supremacy of Christ. And all this vigorous grasp of God's great thought is not only an interpretation of the universe, but it helps wondrously the individual soul to be strong and wax valiant in the fight. Such a man sees that evil is not a trifle, sin not a mere blemish, wrong not the unripe fruit of right. Evil is seen with mighty head and front. The kingdom of wickedness is a tremendous reality. It is organized wrong, intensely active and immensely potent. And sometimes it makes such a praying man afraid. Even Christ "feared." He had his hours of conflict with the power of darkness.

But right over against the kingdom of evil with its Satanic head, and its allegiant spirits, and its willing subjects among men, is the "kingdom of God," Christ its head, its subjects redeemed and rescued and praying and believing souls. And the issue is joined. The praying man takes sides with God. And there is, as the direct result of these views of Christ's kingdom—views, which if not born are yet widened by prayer—the most splendid moral intrepidity.

It is this union of the soul with the great God in prayer, and this alliance of our interests with those of his great "kingdom," that rids many a man of an unutterable and horrible loneliness. There is hardly another oppression so great as that of being morally alone—the sense of being out of sympathy with God, and standing amid pitiless and destructive forces that can so easily wreck us. On a dark night, on some dreary moor, where the thick rain comes in frenzied swirls, and the earth trembles with the jar of the thunder, and the whole world seems at the sport of all mightiest agencies, stands a man, alone, fearfully, terribly alone, with all these adverse powers doing their worst about him. But about prayerless men, whether they see it or not, there is the gathering storm, the loosing of moral elements that can affright the bravest man. Now and then a man's eyes are opened. He sees the danger and is awake to his frightful moral loneliness. Such a one may have another vision, that of God inviting the lonely soul to the companionship of the forgiven and the saved; and, better than all, to fellowship with the Father through Jesus Christ our Lord. To lonely souls comes the call, "draw nigh unto Me." And the one way is that of believing prayer. The new alliance with God is the end of spiritual loneliness.

Prayer as an habitual mood is greatly promoted, again, by the use of set times and special places for its exercise. We are not told, happily, how often to pray. How formalism would then have seized on what is the freest of all things, this matter of prayer! How much of mechanical religion, had we been commanded as to the number of times for prayer and as to its specific places! The freedom left us by our Lord is not the freedom to omit, but the freedom to accept, frequently, the privilege. We are not left to use any place for our closet of prayer because place is of no importance, but for the very opposite reason. Men find that they can do better work in manual labor, better work as students and accountants, when they have become *wonted to places*. The boy was almost a philosopher, who gave as a reason for missing the question, that he was not used to the new school-house. We find that we must have a particular place for our daily devotions. When a lady told her pastor that her place for prayer was the large drawing-room where balls were held, he expressed surprise. But when she told him that neither at morning nor at night could she be alone even in her own room, but that by rising an hour earlier, the drawing-room could be made her closet, he not only ceased to wonder, but rejoiced at the determination of a Christian woman to be alone at some time, and in some place, each day, with her God. "Enter into thy closet, and when thou hast shut the door, pray." It was the word that suited an age which made public worship the substitute for secret devotion. If there be no stated time and no special place, then this duty will be elbowed along by other duties, quite through the day. Habitual devotion is essential to maintaining the spirit of the exercise. It is only a transcendental delusion with which some meet Christ's demand for "entering the closet," by saying "if I am always in the praying mood why do I need set times and places?" Christ knew us best. He said it. That is enough. But men have asked, whether men should pray daily at the regular time, if they find themselves out of mood for the exercise. Will not such a prayer be merely formal? But this is to make the acceptableness of the prayer depend on our feeling about it. The prayer we may think little of, because of its distractions, may be our best prayer. It had at least the outward form of obedience. We gave God the recognition. We gave him at least the words. We tried to pray. Bodily weariness may have been, just for that hour, almost overpowering. But we would have prayed if we could. We obeyed our Lord. He accepted the attempt. Sometimes, too, a light surprises the praying man on his knees, and the listless beginning may have a joyous ending. If we please Satan by omitting the duty once, because not feeling as much in the mood to-day as yesterday, he will see to it that we are more out of the mood to-morrow. By the time it has been twice or thrice omitted the habit of omission is formed, and stated prayer, as a regular exercise, has ceased.

Besides these regular seasons, room must be made for special periods of supplication, the frequency of them depending upon our circumstances, our feeling, and the burdens laid on us. There are gales of grace. The ship may have on board her cargo. Her clearance is made out. Her men stand in their places. She is out in the stream, and swings lazily with the changing tide. But, all this is in vain until the spirits of the air begin to sing high up in her cordage. The flag lifts on the topmast. The sluggish sails, that hung close to the yards, begin to puff out their folds. The ripples run along the side. Every inch of the ship's white-winged canvas is now spread. The anchor is brought home, and the vessel begins to gather headway in the freshening breeze; and by-and-by, under the favoring gale, she leaps from wave to wave, a thing of life and joy. Yet what has she done but use the glad breeze which God sent from the upper air?

There are breathings of God from the highest heavens. They incite in us corresponding breathings of desire to pray. They come to us in the midst of our work, while we walk the street, and in the waking hour of the night. There are instant petitions that spring to the lips, and they will utter themselves. The prayer prays itself. It is hardly ours; for it is not born of self, not offered by act of will. We cannot stop work to go to the closet, nor wait to bow the reverent knee. These "breathings of desire" come on week-days as well as on Sundays. Then it is a joy to pray, a relief to pray. It may be some special truth,— truth that is prayed out on its devotional side; the soul revelling in it with a kind of joyous abandonment. The high solemn justice of God, it may be, awes us and subdues us. We love the white splendor of the throne and adore him that sitteth thereon. The glory of the attribute rises before us and fills the soul with a new sense of righteousness as the supreme thing in the universe. Holiness is so grand and clear and beautiful in God that we are carried away with sacred delight. Or, again, the prayer gathers itself about God's mercy in Jesus Christ; and we are lifted into a sphere of singular altitude, where the opened heart of God is disclosed in his unspeakable self-moved love for man. Or, some human soul going wrong and nearing the final precipice up which there is no climbing, arrests attention, and that man's case stands before us, and prayer is a plea; and, with a promise for an argument, we bring that soul to our prayer-hearing God. But how enumerate these words of prayer, these subjects that rouse its flame, these objects that stir its importunity? The gales of grace blow fresh, and we spread wide every inch of the canvas and mean to make the most of the favored hour. Only it must be noted that these breezes come from above and do not always blow. You cannot set a time and say "now let the wind blow." God's "set times" are facts. "The wind bloweth where it listeth." We must be ready to take the gale. We cannot order up the wind at will. Always some blessing is ready in answer to prayer; but these special gales know no will but that of God. Expected and prayed for they are to be; but, above all, to be used when they begin to blow. A Christian, finding some special ease or access in prayer, surprised by more grace than had been sought, overjoyed at a manifestation that comes when he had reason to expect God's hidings because of his sins, is to take the utmost pains not to disturb the flow, not to check the leading, not to loiter at anchor when the wind is fair and fresh. For, rightly used, these winds waft one well on in the heavenward voyage.

And now comes the question, whither does this praying mood naturally bring its possessor? What will be the result on personal character of this spirit in a man? That it broadens him for human work, that it achieves for him moral character, that it lifts his thoughts into divinest realms, that it not only helps toward the passive Christian virtues, but gives a man moral intrepidity, that it tends powerfully to mould one's whole moral being—these things are obvious. But they are none of them final ends. They are only preparations for something further on and higher up. They can only mean *heaven is for such a soul.* They are prophetic; and no thinking man can doubt that which such a prophecy declares. These things, wrought into the soul itself, are its "meetness for the inheritance of the saints in light."

But what do the same facts prophesy for the future of the human race itself?

The stream of prayer is getting, as the ages go by, to be more full and clear. The river widens with the centuries. The sediment sinks out of sight. The waters steadily become more transparent. The early impurities from the soils of the far-away hills, from the defilements as the river ran past the old cities where men dwelt, no longer color so deeply the waters. The stream is working itself clear, and the healthful flow is a better omen. The banks are getting to be so far apart as to betoken the nearness of the ocean to which, naturally, such a river must run. That there is more praying as well as better praying, is certain. It is, indeed, sometimes asserted that, as men get intelligent they cease to think so much of prayer and to practise it so often. And it is, of course, true, that many a praying boy has become a prayerless man, because he has fed his intellect and starved his soul; exactly as he may have become an invalid in health because he has neglected his body while developing his mind.

This is brain at the expense of soul and of body. There are communities and ages of this sort of man. But nature has her revenges. She knows how to deal with such a man and such an age. Pugilistic families die out; so do merely intellectual families. Nature demands a balance, and gets it, in the long run. She insists that man is a tri-unity. Seen in single families, in single generations, and even in single natures, the moral nature that demands prayer would seem to have a winter time, in which it dies down to the bracts. But spring comes again. The growth, ere it died down in winter, left in each joint a resurrection germ, and each germ has future fructifying power; so that there is more arrangement for life in the fact of apparent death than in any other way. The moral nature comes back to its prominence inevitably; and the thrift of a moral nature is in its prayer. So that prayer is going to multiply. When you can have men's bodies without respiration, and men's minds without thought, you are going to get men born whose moral nature has no promptings to pray. True, some men may do so little with either part of their nature, that you may begin to question its existence. But it is there; suppressed, misused, ignored,—but it is there. It would sometimes seem as if, here and there, a man, judging by his little care for its health, had no body; just as some men and some whole ages have had so little intellectual life, have thought so little, that we are half ready to question whether they have any mind of their own. And so there are some men and some ages, here whole communities, there great nations, which develop for a limited time the intellect at the expense of the soul, and we might almost think that they had none of the devotional cravings of a moral nature. But hybrid ages, like hybrid creatures, run out, by natural law. For moral law is natural law as really as is physical law, and the analogies of the two are striking and instructive. And yet, at certain points, it would seem as if now animalism and now mentalism were the main thing. Nowhere is intellect so flourishing, within its very narrow circle, as when it has almost run its round and come down to death. Seen at that point, it would look as if the more the intelligence the less the prayer. You may find an intellectual son of Anak; but Anakim are sterile and die out. An age, intellectual at the expense of the moral nature, is sure to go under in the struggle for existence; exactly as an age when men have feebler bodies is sure to succumb. Small cycles show men intellectual here, and physically well developed there, without the moral element that voices itself in prayer. But sweep with your glass the larger cycle, and you get indications sure and clear that the true cycle for man and age—the coming man and the ultimate age—is the cycle of the human trinity of body and mind and soul, each with clarified longings, each developed in harmony with the other, all blending in a demand which includes praying as certainly as breathing and thinking. The ultimate man is religious. The ultimate age is prayerful. The final goal is a "sound mind in a sound body" and both dominated by a sound soul. Cycle will work within cycle to the evolution of the prayer. The volume will swell until the river touches the ocean.

And as prayer is more, so it is purer. It must come around, in the cycle, to Eden,—the better Eden of a gospel redemption. Prayer is increasing in quality as well as in quantity. Not, just at this point, are we asking whether there are not better answers to the better prayers of the race; but here and now, the inquiry is concerning the reflex power of this purified body of augmented prayer *upon praying men;* and of what all this means upon the coming ages, in the moral quality of the men who are to do the ultimate praying of the race. The sanctifying power of prayer, as it comes to be a force for human development, is the present point of view. We can see its natural tendency on the individual man. Let any man come to be a thoroughly and an intelligently prayerful man, and it cannot be otherwise than that all his life is touched, even to its outer circumference, by this habit. He is wont to bring all his life into review before his holy God; to mention to him his bodily wants, to ask for preservation when in health and restoration when he is sick; to bring into his closet his chief trials in business, and his infirmities as a man; his sins, asking their forgiveness and pledging himself to struggle against their repetition; his social duties, his political relations, his work as a member of the household of faith, his duty to the ignorant millions at home and abroad—in short, all his relations to God and to man come into review, when he is alone in prayer with his Creator and his Sovereign. Can a man do this, and not be a morally elevated man thereby? Can any considerable number of men do it, and the community not be benefited thereby? Can there be a praying age that is not an approach to an ideal age? Can the race have a great future that does not include prayer in its vast volume and in its clarifying power? The "age to come" must needs be a praying age, if it is to be the age for which the best men hope.

Among the reasons for believing that the race is to see a culminating era of prayer, may be mentioned: First, the yearning therefor, which seems to be a heritage from our old Eden. It is equally a memory and a prophecy; and which it is, at any given hour, depends on whether one is looking backward to Paradise lost, or looking forward to Paradise restored. No man has individual memories of Eden. Nevertheless no one fact in sociology is getting itself to be more universally recognized than the unity of the human race. The facts of heredity show that the race is one as certainly as that every man is one. Heredity conjoined with personality is abundantly acknowledged to-day. The scorning of scorners at the words of the Scripture about the sin of fathers visited on the children, has gone by. Traits of body are transmitted because of the race-bond. Heredity can only be true of a race treated as one. Nor bodily traits only, but mental and moral as well, are transmitted. These inherited peculiarities are seen in the great nations. And closer home, in our social life, who cannot discern them in the various households of our acquaintance? These family markings may overleap one generation, only to reappear subsequently in some individual, in peculiar intensity. Nor are these all evil traits. Some special firmness of conscience, some stalwart trait of character inherited from remote ancestry, stamps a whole series of descendants. You can trace the Huguenot and the Pilgrim. These moral advantages bestowed on a child as the result of a Christian ancestry, are not a substitute for conversion, but they are a direct preparation therefor. In the great world-history, one ancient family, developing afterward into the Hebrew nation, had special religious endowment. Its moral convictions were its strongest convictions. It had a genius for religion. It held the primal traditions. It kept, in some fair measure, the primal beliefs. It was receptive of the truths given when Adam was created in "knowledge." It held in memory, more or less definitely, the original impressions with which God dowered Adam for transmission to the race. The broken plan necessitated a change in the teaching of mankind. And the blur of the primal sin must have confused the subsequent impressions. But some of them were sure to come out along the ages of the progress of the race. Here and there, not only in Jew but in Gentile, some man would have the "vital eye;" some man would snatch a glimpse of the meaning of the primal promise to Adam; some bard would have prophetic vision. These primal impressions went into the stock of the race, and were sure to be revived. These old convictions and hopes, these echoes of Eden, would be transmitted and come to utterance in men of genius:—come not as the result of reasoning, but as the reproduction of dim far-away feelings that craved utterance. They were inborn of the race, and must get voice through finer souls. It is only one form of the doctrine of heredity to hold that the grander traditions, the primitive beliefs, have reappeared in seers and poets. There is no need of failing to recognize the highest flashes of human inspiration. For the Hebrew singers, we claim that over and above their native human inspiration, there was another inspiration, that of God's Holy Spirit. For other seers, we may not claim a divine impulse, but only that through heredity they were made heirs of the traditional hopes of the race. Whenever, on gifted wing, these souls have soared to their highest flights, they have seen a better day for the race. Matthew Arnold's pinion broke when he sung his pessimistic lines. He has sung nothing since. Pessimism cannot sing. Poets are men of hope. The plainest of them can sing of "the good time coming." The loftier of them have a "golden age," an "Elysium" to be gained. "A grand far-off event" is the goal to which vision is turned. Just what it is, they cannot say; for, apart from the Christian faith, they can only see through a glass darkly. But these reminiscences from Paradise, these convictions that an Eden, better than that lost, shall come round again, are certainly noteworthy. They seem almost like "whispers dropt from the heavenly places:" like hints falling out of lips that need only in addition the divine inspiration to speak out concerning the "millennium glory." As the waxing moon draws forth the great waters that flow about all the continents of the world, so these presentient souls have carried about all the centuries of man's severer lot the tides of a better hope, lest the world's heart should break. Had God used reasonings, the world, which has never been a reasoning world, might have missed the teaching. But the oracle and the song, the flash of the loftier thought, the insight of the souls in which feeling is quick and strong, and, over against all these, the waiting of the great congregation of the world for the hopeful word, and its "amen" in the response of all who hear it uttered—these things are immensely significant. True, much of this impression is general in its idea of what the ripe age of the world will be. Absence of certain ills is the glory of the coming age, with some. With others it is a better civilization. Men just out of the bondage of despotism make it consist largely in freedom. Sociologists think of better conditions in which labor and capital, the claims of the body and the soul, and the artificial and real distinctions of life, shall be better adjusted. Men think of a time when war shall cease, when equal rights shall be enjoyed, when intellectual and moral development shall reach the highest stages. They agree, however, in one thing, they look onward. Something better is to come. The ages wait. There is expectation. But when it is to be and in what way the coming crowning age is to be best and grandest, those men who are untouched by a higher than human inspiration cannot say. There is an instructive prophecy in human hearts, as Milton sings, "that time will run back and fetch the age of gold." Shelley calls it the age where "the Paradise Islands gleam." St. Simon has it "that the Golden age is not behind, but before us." Tennyson hopes for a far off time, at last, when peace will come, "and every winter change to spring." Pope will have it true that there comes an age when we shall see

> "Peace o'er the world her olive wand extend,
> And white-robed Innocence from heaven descend;"

And Whittier adds,

> "I fold o'er wearied hands and wait,
> In calm assurance of the good."

Cowper sings,

> "The dwellers in the vales and on the rocks
> Shout to each other, and the mountain tops
> From distant mountains catch the flying joy;
> Till, nation after nation taught the strain,
> Earth rolls the rapturous hosanna round."

Only the age that is devotional as well as practical in its piety, can fill out these yearnings in glad satisfaction.

And, again, the ultimate age may be argued from the aspirations of praying men. Their better devotional moments have in them a kind of prophecy. Such men are led in their prayers. They feel that the Inspirer is the Answerer of their special petition. God has laid the world on some men as a burden. They note every fact that transpires in providence as a hindrance or a help to the final glory. Missionaries are asking that prayer may be concentrated now for this and now for that special feature of their work. Temperance organizations, educational societies, and Y. M. C. associations are requesting that some particular Sabbath or week day shall be devoted to prayer for their specialties. The "Week of Prayer" has obtained a kind of recognition in the religious calendar of many churches. And a "day of prayer for Colleges" is observed by the more intelligent Christians of the nation. In the service of all these days, there is the onward glance, the prophetic hope. The nearer thing is the specific object, but always there is the reference to the larger aim and broader expectation of a redeemed world.

This profound impression of praying men is not precisely what we should, at first, naturally expect. For, each of these men looks for final and *personal salvation in heaven*. He was consciously "saved" when converted. He has assurance of "eternal life" for himself. He has put salvation just where our Lord places it, as the direct outcome of personal faith. He believed unto salvation. He took Christ as his own Saviour. He has grasped the promise, "He that believeth on the Son hath everlasting life;" and he sees that this means heaven, and does not at all require a golden age for the human race on earth in the distant future. In point of fact some good men have either denied or ignored the world's conversion in the coming age; so unlike are the spiritual salvation of a soul and the prevalence on earth of "Christ's kingdom." That the latter should have been so pressed upon praying men in their best devotional hours, that some have so enjoyed the holy prospect of a time when the nations of the world shall be under the sway of Christ, must be looked upon as a kind of prophetic intimation given to those who live much in communion with God. Indeed, some good men do not know the full meaning of their own prayers. Keble sings,

> "And if some tone be false or low,
> What are all prayers beneath
> But cries of babes that cannot know
> Half the deep thought they breathe?"

And this intercessory prayer—prayer for others—which is used so often by the great believers, in the Bible story, and which has been alike model and inspiration for good men in all ages, has nearly always the onward glance; and it grows stronger for the special victory by the remembrance of the final conquest of God.

There stands out on the sacred page as one of the grandest triumphs of Prayer, the case of Moses. God was about to destroy the people. Moses, type of the Great Intercessor, prays that he will not do it. "Blot me, also, out of thy book." He obtains mercy toward the people. But God said that he himself could not go as their Leader in the journey through the wilderness. He would send his angel in his stead. Moses is in agony. "If thou go not with me carry us not up hence." He had rather die than not have God with the people. And again and again in those long and weary years of the wandering, Moses prayed for the people, and pleaded for them the promise of God. But in urging, in prayer, what has been called the "great Rest Promise" of the Bible, he used but a part of it in his plea for Israel. It meant the "Rest" of the further ages. For the "Rest Promise" was repeated in David's time; it not having been exhausted when Joshua entered Canaan. It reappeared in Paul's time. It comes out again in the "Revelation" of John. It finds its greatest application, of course, in the heavenly world. "There remaineth," *i.e.*, it remaineth true, "there remaineth therefore a rest to the people of God." But while there is a heavenly, there is included in this unexpected rest-promise an earthly blessing. And in the great argument of his prayers, Moses uses the plea of what will the nations be likely to say if Israel is left of her God, and also the plea of God's own glory among all the people. Moses feels that he is acting on the theatre of the world, and the drama is to culminate in the further ages. Samuel was, likewise, an intercessor, asking for the near, but having his eye on the cause of his God. Elijah was conspicuously a prophet of national life, and used his powers of intercession for results beyond the immediate surroundings of his personal career. Consciously or unconsciously he was acting in such a way that, far off, in New Testament times, he should be quoted as an example of a righteous man whose prayer avails with God. David's prayers and songs have in them the foregleam. So, too, have the great prophets, as they see the glory of the Lord filling the whole earth. But it is in the Epistles of Paul that the thought culminates; and his broadening vision embraces not only salvation for the individual saint, but salvation for the ages as well. These great human intercessors lift prayers for the world that are to bring abundant answers. But the chief reason for looking for an age, one of the main characteristics of which is its happy prayerful communion with God, is the express declaration of the Sacred Scriptures.

Let it be at once granted that a large number of Old Testament verses often quoted in support of this position, are not direct proof texts. Let us yield the point to the critics, that verses, like those in Isaiah, about the "Lord's House as established on the top of the mountains, and all nations shall flow unto it," had their literal fulfilment in the restoration from the Captivity and the rebuilding of the Temple at Jerusalem; and that they had the beginning of their *spiritual* fulfilment in the gospel day, at the Pentecostal gathering. But if this be granted, there is still a prophetic trend to the words. They have outlook. There is the vital glance in them. If it were too much to claim from such declarations a literal restoration of Jerusalem, it is not too much to see in them a glimpse of an age that shall be a better restoration than that would be. The full type shall be a restored Eden rather than a restored Jerusalem. But the old glory of Jerusalem rebuilt, shall help us by its suggestiveness. The great glory is not of a coming earthly city, but of a coming earthly age. As with one so with dozens of similar verses written before the Restoration. For the historic view and the prophetic differ as do the two views of a mountain range. History stands before the range, counts the mountain heads and names them separately and gives the width of the valleys between them. Prophecy goes around to the end of the range and sees the hill tops only. From this point, the valleys disappear. The hills blend into one. They are in the same line of vision. To see the near is to see also the more distant. The trend of the events is the prophetic vision of them—their connection, not especially in point of time, but in similarity of character. Any doom seen, has a glance onward to the final doom; any salvation has Christ's salvation in view; any restoration sees also a restored age; and the blessing of a "spirit of grace and supplication" sees also the final age of man's "communion with God."

But the wonderful Second Psalm, a Sacred Drama, is a direct unfolding of God's plan of a final glory of the world. It is not, here, a prophet politically concerned for the fortunes of a single city, but a seer looking out on the ages. God is one of the *dramatis personæ*. He bids the Son, another of the persons, who is seated on a holy hill, to ask of him, according to an arrangement, the whole heathen world for a possession. God would dwell among the nations. If some will not let him rule, they are to be destroyed; but there shall be vast multitudes who accept his reign.

The ultimate ages shall be allegiant to God. Therefore, kings are exhorted to enter into the closest relation to Christ. And the drama closes with the words of blessing on the men of the ages to come who put their trust in the Lord. It is the Psalm that sees, through the nearer din, the peace of the final age of communion with Christ. Daniel saw the "Stone that filled the whole earth," and said that unto the Son of Man "was given dominion and glory and a kingdom, that all people, nations, and languages should serve him." And the parables of the growth of "the kingdom" given by our Lord, have this far-away air. The grain of mustard seed has no end of expanding. The leaven leavens, at length, all the meal.

And this has not been true of all individuals, and cannot be true of all the past members of the race. It can be argued as true only of those living in the final age. Or if it be understood as a "parable of trend rather than as a parable of result," there is no mistaking the direction of the trend. In that age, all nations are to serve the Lord and to come and worship before him. The same great fact of a coming age is to be held, whether one interprets the millennial utterances mathematically or metaphorically; whether one believes in a post-millennium or a pre-millennium, in any millennium or in no millennium at all. All that it is here necessary to maintain is that an age is coming to which so much of the world's prayer has looked, for which it has been a preparation and in which it culminates. But of all the glowing writers who have seen the better age and foretold its characteristic of happy devotion, none can equal in grasp of thought or swift-winged accuracy of word the apostle Paul. He revels "in the ages to come," or as his words might be given "in the ages that are coming on." The idea is of a grand succession, interrupted it may be here and there, but still on the whole advancing toward the age of ages, when all will have "come on." It is "the dispensation of the fulness of times" toward which he is looking.

He sees Christ the inheritor of the ages, as the older and dimmer prophets saw him as having an inheritance among the nations. The ages, in the glowing conception of the first part of his Epistle to the Ephesians, are Christ's heritage; being a purchased possession. And all redeemed men then living, and all those who, at an earlier time than the Ephesians had first heard the gospel, constitute a part of the new redeemed age—an age which was to have such grand succession of ages when all things were to be summed up in Christ. And therefore it is that Paul says he "makes mention of them," in this age-relation, "in his prayers," so that they also may see more clearly the glory of Christ's inheritance in the ages. All this is not heaven; it is earth. It is not the glory of the skies but of the "ages to come," "in the fulness of the dispensation of times." He sees, further on in the same Epistle, the Gentile world becoming "fellow-heirs." And he continues: "For this cause I bow my knees unto the Father." In other Epistles the same idea is always emerging. In some of them the fervor of his soul interrupts the flow of his argument, and the broad, strong, victorious conception of the ultimate age bursts forth here in doxology and there in glad and glowing prayer. "Now unto him that is able to do exceeding abundantly above all that we ask or think, according to the power that worketh in us,—unto him be the glory in the Church through all ages, world without end." Nor is this final clause a mere collection of synonomous words. It is given in the margin of the Revised Version, "age of ages." In such an "age of ages" the prayer may differ little, in many respects, from the praise. It may not be without petition, but it will abound in ascription and thanksgiving.

It must be understood that the inquiry is not now about the victory of the Church; that is assured. Or about the success of organized Christianity over all religions; that is guaranteed. Nor is it the question about a time when every man on the planet will be a Christian disciple. It is the rather a recognition of a trend, the culmination of prophetic feeling and of Scripture intimation. It is the expectation of an "age to come," the age of the ages, when literature and law, the tone of human sentiment, the "spirit of the time," the lines of popular thought, the active convictions and the settled principles of men, shall be thoroughly, and therefore devotionally, Christian; when the arts and sciences and habits of life, the employments and recreations of mankind shall be ennobled by a consciousness of God above and eternity before them; when thought shall be run in Christian moulds; when faith in God and so in good men shall cast out doubt and distrust; when prayer to God shall be natural and universal; when the human capacity for loving shall be so enlarged by the loving of God that men shall love each other with holy love, thus lifting an instinct to the rank of a religious virtue; when work shall be worship and the prayer of the lip in the closet shall act itself out all day long in the prayer of the life. That would be the age of prayer and of all else that goes naturally and happily therewith. For there is no duty of the state or the household, of the church or the school, of the public or the private life, that is not enriched by a devotional piety. And when such enrichment and enlargement become the persuasive and animating spirit of mankind, then will be shown the fact that the Christianity which can save an individual can *save also an age.*

How this will be brought about we may not say. We simply mark the trend, and call attention to the prophecy it holds in itself. This only is to be said: that nothing in the moral universe of God is so strong, so sure, so set upon reaching its final goal, as a moral trend.

In some aspects of present moral movement, it would seem that the "age of ages" was very far off and very slow in coming on. Gigantic wrongs still raise their head and are loud in their claim. Political and social and religious errors abound. The foes are able and unscrupulous. But God has all the forces of the world in his hands. He lets them at times do their worst. He manages them when they seem most free. He lets the eddy flow backward, but the law of the river is that it runs onward and downward; its very volume and direction is what makes the eddy near the shore. God keeps accounts. God times events. Just so many defeats of a wise measure, before it is possible to enact it. The defeats all count toward the result. Just so many drops of blood from a slave's back, the very last one of them necessary, and the time comes for Emancipation. Just one more turn of the screw of Roman despotism, and Christ is born. The process, from this point of view, seems steady and slow. It is the favorite one of many because, just now, scientists are making prominent the facts that show development to be a law. But it is coming to be seen that there may be development through sudden introduction of forces sometimes destructive and sometimes saving. In nature we have the sun slowly rising and steadily mounting the sky, and we have, as well, the instant flash of the lightning splintering the oak that had used a century of the best sunshine.

Moral catastrophes and salvations are sometimes as strangely sudden for single souls, and for single ages. We read of nations to be morally "born in a day," as we see them sometimes politically springing up into life in an instant of time. What God has in reserve, what concentration of human prayer and effort, on which the power of mighty moral miracle is to rest, who can say? All moral reformation heretofore has begun and culminated in prayer. The energy, pervasive as is the light that so many use always and seldom recognize, which enters into all Christian effort and moulds it and brings it into harmony with the will and work of God, is that of the *prayers of prayerful men.*

> "More things are wrought by prayer
> Than this world dreams of. Wherefore let thy voice
> Rise like a fountain for me night and day.
> For what are men better than sheep or goats
> That nourish a blind life within the brain,
> If, knowing God, they lift not hands of prayer,
> Both for themselves, and those who call them friend.
> For so the whole round world is every way
> Bound by gold chains about the feet of God."

www.ingramcontent.com/pod-product-compliance
Lightning Source LLC
Chambersburg PA
CBHW031729230426
43669CB00007B/299